G000146889

THE OFFICIAL ENGLAND RUGBY BOOK

RUGBY WORLD CUP 2015 EDITION

England
Rugby

First published by Carlton Books Limited in 2015

Carlton Books Limited
20 Mortimer Street
London W1T 3JW

A CIP catalogue record for this book is available from the British Library.
10 9 8 7 6 5 4 3 2 1

ISBN 978-1-78097-663-1

Project Editor: Matt Lowing
Project Art Editor: Luke Griffin
Picture Researcher: Paul Langan
Book designer: Darren Jordan
Editorial: Caroline Curtis and Chris Parker
Production: Maria Petalidou

Printed in Spain

All statistics correct as of April 2015

THE OFFICIAL ENGLAND RUGBY BOOK

RUGBY WORLD CUP 2015 EDITION

Julian Bennetts

CARLTON BOOKS

Twickenham Stadium – the biggest Rugby-dedicated ground in the world – has played host to many memorable England Rugby performances

Contents

Foreword by Stuart Lancaster

England Rugby

When I was appointed England Head Coach on a full-time basis the role was multi-layered.

Firstly, we had to win back public confidence in the side. Secondly we had to build a strong culture within the squad. Thirdly, we had to forge attacking and defensive structures that could be effective against the very best sides in the world.

I can confidently say we have done all of those things.

The players, coaches and management team carry the expectations of the country on our shoulders. It is a privilege and honour.

We all remember where we were when Jonny Wilkinson kicked that drop-goal in 2003 and the effect it had on the country. We all know what it would mean if we could do something similar this time.

That is the aim, and I am confident we can be successful.

We will not be able to do it without your support though. I often think back to Euro '96 and the way England united behind Terry Venables' side. The atmosphere was electric, on the streets as well as in the stadiums. That is what we need, and that is what you can provide.

Of course, this Tournament stretches beyond the England team. The best players and the best teams in the world will be on our shores, and from Exeter to Newcastle the rugby will be tremendous.

We hope that the next few weeks will leave a legacy that benefits the entire country.

But when it comes to our prospects of achieving our goal and winning the Tournament at Twickenham on October 31 we need your support.

We require your help, be it in the stadium, in your local club, or at home.

Thank you

Stuart Lancaster chats with his captain Chris Robshaw after England defeated Australia at Twickenham Stadium in November 2014

Chris Robshaw 32nd Cap 1316
England v Australia
29th N...

Introduction

Twenty unions, 620 players, 48 matches, 13 venues, millions of spectators worldwide, but just one winner. Finally Rugby World Cup 2015 is here.

It is 144 years since England played its first rugby union international, but winning Rugby World Cup 2015 on home soil would outstrip any of the triumphs or achievements that have gone before.

From the early days, when six Grand Slams were won between 1913 and 1928, to the latter-day triumphs and that famous Rugby World Cup Final victory in 2003, there are many moments that would demand inclusion in a discussion of England's finest victories.

But winning Rugby World Cup 2015 at Twickenham Stadium on October 31 would be a clear contender. Head Coach Stuart Lancaster's regime has regained the faith of the public and they will not lack for fervent, feverish support during what will be a stunning seven weeks.

Lancaster has built a side to be reckoned with, combining youthful exuberance and strong leaders.

But to win the Tournament they will have to beat the best, and they are well aware the cream of world Rugby is arriving on these shores over the next few weeks.

Everyone has their favourite Rugby World Cup moment. For some it is Jonny Wilkinson's drop goal in 2003, for others France's epic victories over New Zealand. It could be when Tonga shocked France in 2011 or when Wales lost to Fiji four years previously. Then

think of youngsters exploding on to the stage, as Takudzwa Ngwenya did when he roared past Bryan Habana in the 2007 Tournament, or old stagers enjoying one last glorious moment in the sun such as Mario Ledesma in 2011. Alternatively, it could be a moment you know simply matters, as when Nelson Mandela presented Francois Pienaar with the Webb Ellis Cup in 1995.

One thing we do know for sure is that Rugby World Cup 2015 will create new memories, new heroes and moments to remember.

Few Tournaments have been as keenly anticipated as this one. The story four years ago was all about New Zealand, the union looking to exorcise the ghosts of every Tournament since 1987 by winning the Webb Ellis Cup for the first time since the inaugural event. They managed it – just – beating France by a solitary point in a brutal arm-wrestle.

Richie McCaw and friends are still the team to beat. Losing a match every two years on average, they will be confident of becoming the first team to retain their Rugby World Cup crown.

The other Southern Hemisphere sides will be confident, too. South Africa have a typically belligerent pack and some hugely talented backs with many tipping fly-half Handré Pollard to be one of the stars of the Tournament.

Australia are rebuilding but with the likes of Israel Folau, Adam Ashley-Cooper and Tevita Kuridrani in their squad they can never be discounted.

But the challenge from the Northern Hemisphere will be fierce. Wales, particularly at the Millennium Stadium, are a force to be reckoned with. France are capable of anything, Scotland are improving and Ireland are a team transformed by Joe Schmidt. Then we come to the host union, England, who certainly have a chance of winning it.

Whoever is victorious, it promises to be a spectacular Tournament where new stars will rise. In 2011 Aaron Cruden was not even a member of the New Zealand squad, but after an injury to Dan Carter he came through to start the Final. Even then the story was not done, as an injury to Cruden brought Stephen Donald to the fore. He kicked the winning penalty, and his name is now part of New Zealand rugby folklore.

So whether you support an underdog or follow a union that expects to be at Twickenham Stadium on October 31, clear your schedule for mid-September and all of October. It is going to be a Tournament you don't want to miss.

The Webb Ellis Cup – international Rugby's greatest prize – awaits the winner of Rugby World Cup 2015

England
Rugby

England Expects

The time for waiting is over. Now we find out whether England can win the Tournament for the first time since 2003, and the first time on home soil in their history.

Focused and ready for anything,
England in action against Australia
at Twickenham Stadium in 2014

England Expects

England
Rugby

By the time England kick off Rugby World Cup 2015 against Fiji it will have been 4,015 days since Jonny Wilkinson's drop goal won the 2003 Final. The anticipation has been building, and now it's time to deliver.

Seven weeks from immortality.

Seven matches from greatness.

Seven long weeks of intensity, physical and mental exhaustion and unrelenting pressure.

But what a prize at the end of it. The chance for Chris Robshaw, George Ford, Dan Cole and the rest to put their names alongside those of Jonny Wilkinson, Martin Johnson, Mike Catt and the boys of 2003. The chance to call themselves world champions.

It is an event all rugby fans have been waiting for since July 28, 2009. That was the day the IRB officially announced England would host Rugby World Cup 2015, adding to what we already knew would be the UK's Golden Decade of Sport.

The Olympic Games were glorious. The Rugby League World Cup, two Ryder Cups and the Commonwealth Games, also. We know the UK can stage magnificent sporting events – and now England rugby fans want

to find out if their union can win a Tournament as well as host one.

The players Stuart Lancaster will select know this is a life-changing opportunity for them. Mo Farah, Bradley Wiggins and Jessica Ennis-Hill know what it's like to triumph in front of their adoring home fans, but England's rugby players will instead be looking to emulate the achievements of 12 years ago.

The Final will be held at Twickenham Stadium on October 31,

"When I think of England at its best in sport ... there is no better feeling ... I remember Euro '96 vividly, particularly the sense of identity. We want to replicate that emotion and intensity."

England Head Coach, Stuart Lancaster

Right: Fly-half George Ford has produced a number of impressive performances for England

Opposite: England line up to sing the national anthem at Twickenham Stadium in 2014

The England players huddle to discuss match tactics. To be victorious, England must combine tactical acumen with thrilling, powerful rugby

and if England are crowned Rugby World Cup 2015 winners on that day in south-west London, they will become national heroes.

We know what to expect from that heady return from Australia in 2003, or England's victorious Ashes-winning side two years later. The question is whether they can do it. The short answer, undoubtedly, is yes. There are members of this England side – Courtney Lawes, Joe Launchbury, Dan Cole, Mike Brown – who could very easily have pushed for inclusion in a World XV over the last couple of years. Marrying that with fervent home support will make for a potent combination.

Lancaster has had to forge a side in his own image since succeeding Martin Johnson after Rugby World Cup 2011, initially on a temporary basis before making an unarguable case that he deserved the job full-time.

He has tapped into the history of the England team, ensuring these players are well aware of the footsteps in which they walk. He has instilled a sense of brotherhood which few sides in the world are able to match. He has attempted to recalibrate what it means to play for England; the pride it gives your family, the lengths to which you will go in order to defend the shirt and your honour. The culture of

Above: Forward Courtney Lawes contributes powerful runs and huge tackles to England. He is a player who could easily push for inclusion in a World XV

Opposite: Anthony Watson's deft ball-handling skills and pace helped him to score two tries for England in 2015

the team is strong, built on solid foundations.

"The more you have to play for, the better you play," is one of his key tenets.

Yet as the Cumbrian schoolteacher well knows, that counts for nothing if you don't have the players capable of defeating Northern or Southern Hemisphere rivals. He put his stall out early, trusting youth.

In his first act as Head Coach, Lancaster made a statement. By appointing Robshaw captain he knew what he was getting: an honesty and whole-heartedness that encapsulated the approach he wanted. He followed that with bold selection choices, eschewing tried and tested for young and fearless. There have been setbacks, as you would expect, but there have also been glorious successes.

Take Owen Farrell. A debutant in Lancaster's first match in charge, he is now a proven Test animal, and a threat to any side in the world. The same goes for Launchbury, Joe Marler or the Vunipola brothers.

The moment we knew what this side was capable of came against New Zealand in November 2012. The Southern Hemisphere union were unbeaten in 20 matches but were blown away by what Matt Dawson described as "maybe the greatest England victory, ever, at Twickenham".

It changed what we expected from England, and ensured they would go into Rugby World Cup 2015 knowing how to beat the side that are favourites for the Webb Ellis Cup.

It immediately raised England's profile under Lancaster and made them genuine contenders. That impression has continued with wins

over every major Rugby nation bar South Africa and three close-run contests in the Six Nations.

True, England were themselves blown away in Cardiff in the final match of 2013, but they learnt an invaluable lesson about the power of unity. That day, it felt like England were not playing against 15 men in red but an entire nation desperate to ensure they didn't have to watch their oldest adversaries triumphing on their soil. They also showed a more expansive side of their game in the tournament just gone.

Lancaster has talked of the greatest sporting moments in England's history, particularly of the heady days of Euro '96 and the way the country came together.

"When I think of England at its best in sport – during Euro '96 or

"There are a lot of players in the changing room who have now played in big games ... That investment in the last two to three years is beginning to tell."

England Head Coach, Stuart Lancaster

when they're doing well in cricket – there is no better feeling," he said early in 2014. "I remember Euro '96 vividly, particularly the sense of identity. We want to replicate that emotion and intensity."

Yet they have to negotiate a tough pool even to make the knockout stages, with Wales, Australia, Fiji and Uruguay providing a stiff test. Survive that though, and England will be battle-hardened.

They will need the pack to fire, as they have done consistently under the shrewd guidance of Graham Rowntree, who continued the fine work he had performed as assistant coach under Johnson. The backs, led by Andy Farrell and Mike Catt, are clearly improving. In George Ford, Anthony Watson and Jonathan Joseph they have three young tyros who could be household names before the year is out.

They will wonder if they have had enough time to prepare and gel, and they will fret over whether their combinations will fire or their set-pieces will be up to the task.

But the time for waiting is at an end. The time for asking questions is over, and it is time for answers.

England expects and this is their chance. Immortality is just seven steps away.

England
Rugby

Rugby World Cup 2015 Pool A Preview

So this is it. Six years after it was announced England will host Rugby World Cup 2015, they prepare to kick off against Fiji. It is a tough pool though, and here we profile the sides England will come up against.

England scrum-half Ben Youngs in action at Rugby World Cup 2011. He will be looking to add to his Tournament appearances in 2015

Introduction

Australia, England, Wales, Fiji and Uruguay, welcome to one of the most closely matched pools of Rugby World Cup 2015. This will undoubtedly be one of the most fascinating and closely fought pools of the Tournament.

When the draw for Rugby World Cup 2105 was made in London it presented a very tough scenario for the unions in Pool A. England, Wales and Australia in the same pool meant a devilishly tough start to the Tournament for all three of the heavyweights.

When Fiji came through to take their place the level of difficulty went up another notch, with Uruguay the last to secure their place in the Tournament, and in Pool A.

It will certainly be difficult to predict which of the heavyweights will progress to the knockout stages or indeed, if Fiji will.

Stuart Lancaster said at the time it was "definitely a tough pool", while he thought it was fate that his side were drawn against Wales.

Australia will fancy their chances despite having to travel to Twickenham and Cardiff for what are likely to be the decisive matches in the pool.

England will kick off the entire Tournament against Fiji at Twickenham Stadium on Friday, September 18 and it is likely to be a physical contest. England will have to cope with everything thrown at them up front before – they hope – demonstrating their class in a manner similar to their impressive victory over the same opposition in 2012.

Then comes Wales. Lions who bonded together two years ago will be sworn enemies, and the margins are likely to be tighter than ever.

Survive that, and England – whose pool matches after Fiji all kick off at 8pm on Saturday evenings – have the small matter of Australia to attend to. Always a tight and tense affair, England will look to win the battle up front and keep a talented back division quiet by not allowing Israel Folau, Adam Ashley-Cooper and the rest good-quality ball with which to work.

Finally, it is a trip away from Twickenham and up to Manchester. On their last visit to the city England beat Argentina 37–15 in 2009, but that came at Old Trafford; on this occasion they will travel to the east of the city and Manchester City Stadium. There they will face a dangerous Uruguay side who cannot be underestimated after beating Russia to reach this stage.

Rugby World Cup pools do not come any tougher than this. England will be in the thick of the action straight away and it is a mouthwatering prospect.

England are placed in a highly competitive pool at Rugby World Cup 2015. They will have to be at the top of their Game if they are to progress

"It is a tough pool, but if you are going to lift the Webb Ellis Cup you are going to have to win big games and you cannot go into it fearing anybody."

England Head Coach, Stuart Lancaster

England v Fiji

The match that kicks off the whole Tournament is vital for England. Fiji will be physical and committed, but victory is a must.

On Friday, September 18, under the lights at Twickenham Stadium, this is where it all begins.

England have long known this is where their Rugby World Cup 2015 journey would start, but Fiji secured their place only in June 2014 when they, unsurprisingly, crushed the Cook Islands 108–6 in their qualifying match in the Oceania region.

This will be Fiji's seventh appearance in eight Rugby World Cups. Packed full of experienced, powerful players, this side will be no easy ride for England.

Their captain, Akapusi Qera, spent seven years at Gloucester and to give a sign of his pedigree he was voted third in the Premiership Player of the Season Awards in 2007/08. In the backs, Vereniki Goneva and Asaeli Tikoirotuma will be familiar to English audiences. The former was named Players' Player of the Year in 2014 for his stunning displays for Leicester Tigers, while the latter has made a fine start to life on the wing at Harlequins.

It is also worth keeping an eye on Nemani Nadolo, who can play centre or wing. Standing at 1.95m and

weighing 130kg, he is hard to miss, and he scored all of Fiji's points in their encouraging 17–13 defeat to Wales in November 2014.

In the pack Fiji have the wonderfully named Campese Ma'afu (and yes, he really was named after the Australian wing) to call on, while Leone Nakarawa has impressed at lock for Glasgow Warriors.

Yet England will be confident of continuing their proud record of never having lost to Fiji. The last meeting between the two was in November 2012 when England ran

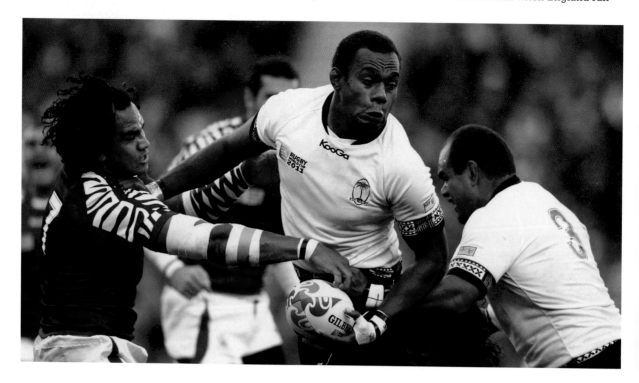

in seven tries in a comprehensive 55–12 victory. That was the first time they had met in 13 years and Stuart Lancaster will be hoping for the same outcome again.

Fiji, though, will be looking to revive the spirit of Rugby World Cup 2007. In France they were one of the stories of the Tournament, beating Wales 38–34 in their final pool match to reach the quarter-finals. There they played South Africa and gave the eventual champions a huge scare, drawing level with 15 minutes to play before going down 37–20.

England cannot afford to underestimate them.

Opposite: England are likely to face Fiji's powerful lock Leone Nakarawa at Rugby World Cup 2015

Above: Vereniki Goneva plays centre or wing and played at Rugby World Cup 2011

Right: England overcame Fiji 54–12 in 2012. They will be looking to kick off Rugby World Cup 2015 with a similar win

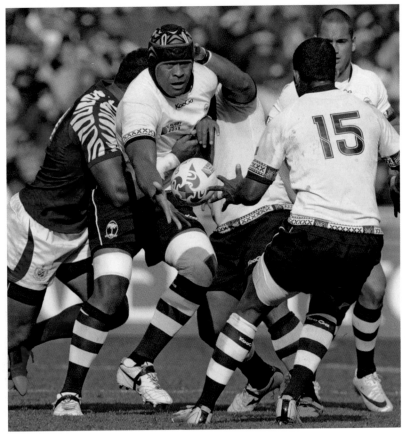

England v Wales

Warren Gatland's side will provide an acid test of England's Rugby World Cup 2015 credentials in just their second match of the Tournament.

England against Wales is not a match for the faint-hearted. Think of seismic collisions at the Millennium Stadium, brutal encounters at Twickenham Stadium and that famous Rugby World Cup 2003 quarter-final in Brisbane. All set the pulse racing.

It is a rivalry that began back on February 19, 1881 when the two sides met at Mr Richardson's field in Blackheath. England won by seven goals – one dropped goal and six tries – to nil. The score was 30–0, although by current scoring standards it would have been far more.

Wales did not beat England until 1890, but the two sides have remained remarkably even ever since. Of the 126 matches played between them, England have won 58, Wales 56 and 12 have been draws – with the last of those being England's Six Nations win in 2015.

Both have enjoyed memorable victories in the modern era too. Wales will proudly point to two efforts that denied England Grand Slams, first at Wembley in 1999 and then in Cardiff in 2013.

England, for their part, can crow about that victory in Rugby World Cup 2003 and their win in Cardiff in 2011, the first time they had won in the Welsh capital in eight years.

Rugby World Cup 2015 however, is a fiendishly more difficult encounter to predict.

Wales have won twice at Twickenham Stadium in recent years and will look to their strike runners – Jamie Roberts, Alex Cuthbert and George North – to help continue that record. Adding another layer of intrigue is the fact the coaches know each other so well, with Andy Farrell and Graham Rowntree assisting Wales boss Warren Gatland during the 2013 Lions tour of Australia.

There are intriguing match-ups all over the field too, with none more keenly anticipated than that between the two No.7s, Chris Robshaw and Sam Warburton. These two captains like to lead by example, so the battle between them will be key.

The front row contest will be brutal, while at lock Joe Launchbury and Courtney Lawes will have to be on their game against whichever pairing Gatland selects from Alun Wyn Jones, Luke Charteris, Jake Ball and Bradley Davies.

Boasting almost an entire Lions back division from Mike Phillips to Leigh Halfpenny, Wales will be strong if they get quick ball. England will need to disrupt them at the breakdown.

Indeed, there is enough talent on show for this to be a fitting Final. It will surely be one of the matches of the Tournament.

Opposite: Wales finished fourth in Rugby World Cup 2011 and will be tough opponents at Rugby World Cup 2015

Above: Tough and uncompromising, Wales captain Sam Warburton has been one of the most consistent players in world Rugby in recent years. He will be looking to drive Wales to their first Rugby World Cup Final

England
Rugby

England v Australia

The repeat of the 2003 Final could be a knockout match this time around. England will have to be at their best against a dangerous Australian side.

Left: The early meeting of these two famous rivals in the pool stages of Rugby World Cup 2015 makes this a mouthwatering fixture. Quade Cooper is one of Australia's most-experienced players and is a major threat to England

Opposite: Australia have a proud Rugby World Cup record and are major contenders to win Rugby World Cup 2015

Opposite, below: For England to overcome Australia it will mean keeping a watchful eye on players such as Australian captain Stephen Moore

So far, we'll call it even.

Australia can look back on the Final of Rugby World Cup 1991, which they won at Twickenham Stadium against their hosts. England can remember their famous victory in the Final of Rugby World Cup 2003, this time in Sydney and once more against the hosts. England also knocked Australia out of Rugby World Cup 1995 and 2007, while Australia got the better of them all the way back in 1987.

But there will be few England–Australia matches which are more keenly anticipated than this one.

Considering the pool, it could well be the equivalent of a last-16 tie – the loser preparing to exit the Tournament, the winner looking forward to the last eight.

Recent history would suggest England may be favourites on home soil, but we all know form counts for little in a Rugby World Cup. England have beaten Australia in three of their last four matches at Twickenham Stadium, but the Southern Hemisphere side's victory

in 2012 was instructive as they soaked up pressure before striking through Nick Cummins.

Under the new leadership of Michael Cheika, Australia will be unpredictable and the challenge will be whether they can unleash their stunning potential in a hugely talented back division.

England will be confident of supremacy up front but aware of the dangers that lurk behind.

Expect much talk of 1991 and 2003 too. For those of you who have

forgotten, England attempted to play a more expansive, open game in the 1991 Final than they had displayed in the Tournament to date but came up short, going down 12–6. Prop Tony Daly scored the only try and Nick Farr-Jones lifted the Trophy triumphantly.

It was a very different story 12 years later. The memories are still fresh, from Jason Robinson's try, to Mike Tindall's tackle on George Gregan, Matt Dawson's sniping run and Jonny Wilkinson's drop goal. What England would give for a repeat performance!

In fact, what they would give for a repeat of 2007! There, in the heat of Marseille, Andrew Sheridan produced the performance of his life and England's scrum proved decisive. Wilkinson kicked four penalties and England went on to reach the Final.

Now they know that victory is vital, no matter how it is achieved. It should be another titanic battle, but one England will hope to edge.

England Rugby

England v Uruguay

England's final match in Manchester could be key to their progress as they search for victory against the South Americans.

England and Uruguay have recent sporting history having played each other in the 2014 FIFA World Cup, but it might be unwise to think for too long about Luis Suárez and the events in São Paulo.

Instead, Stuart Lancaster and his coaching staff would do well to look back to 2003, when England produced one of their most complete performances in Rugby World Cup history. They scored 17 tries against Uruguay in their final pool match in Brisbane, with Josh Lewsey claiming five of them. The 111–13 victory was England's highest ever Rugby World Cup score and helped to bolster the side's confidence before the knockout stages.

England will hope history repeats itself here, this time at Manchester City Stadium. Yet Los Teros cannot be underestimated, as proven by the fact they knocked out Russia in their Rugby World Cup 2015 play-off to reach the Tournament.

Trailing by one point from the first leg, Uruguay ended up 57–49 winners on aggregate after the second match in Montevideo, to spark wild scenes in front of a 14,000 capacity crowd.

Scrum-half Agustín Ormaechea, who scored one of his side's three tries in that second leg, described victory as "an unbelievable feeling" and many neutrals will hope they do well.

Ormaechea is not the first member of his family to compete in the

Tournament either, his father, Diego, becoming the oldest player in Rugby World Cup history when he played in 1999 aged 40.

Uruguay beat Spain that year, and overcame Georgia four years later before that mammoth defeat to England finished off their chances.

Uruguay, with 5,500 registered players, will be coached by ex-Bristol prop Pablo Lemoine – who scored against England in that meeting back in 2003.

Of the squad that played against Russia four members ply their trade in Europe. One of the most exciting of them is fly-half Felipe Berchesi,

who plays for Union Sportive Carcassonnaise in France. He scored 21 points in Uruguay's Rugby World Cup 2015 play-off match against Russia in Montevideo and will be vital to Uruguay's hopes at the Tournament.

Uruguay's lock Franco Lamanna plays in Italy with Perugia while Agustín Ormaechea is based in France and plays for Stade Montois.

For Uruguay, plunged into the toughest of all Rugby World Cup 2015 pools, a single victory would be a huge achievement. England will hope they don't suffer the same fate as the country's football team.

Above: With such highly rated players as Uruguay's Felipe Berchesi against them, England can not afford to be complacent when the unions meet in their pool match

Left: Uruguay will be a force to be reckoned with at Rugby World Cup 2015. Qualification was secured with a 57-49 repechage aggregate victory over Russia

"The boost supporters give players cannot be underestimated and they really are a 16th man."

England Head Coach, Stuart Lancaster

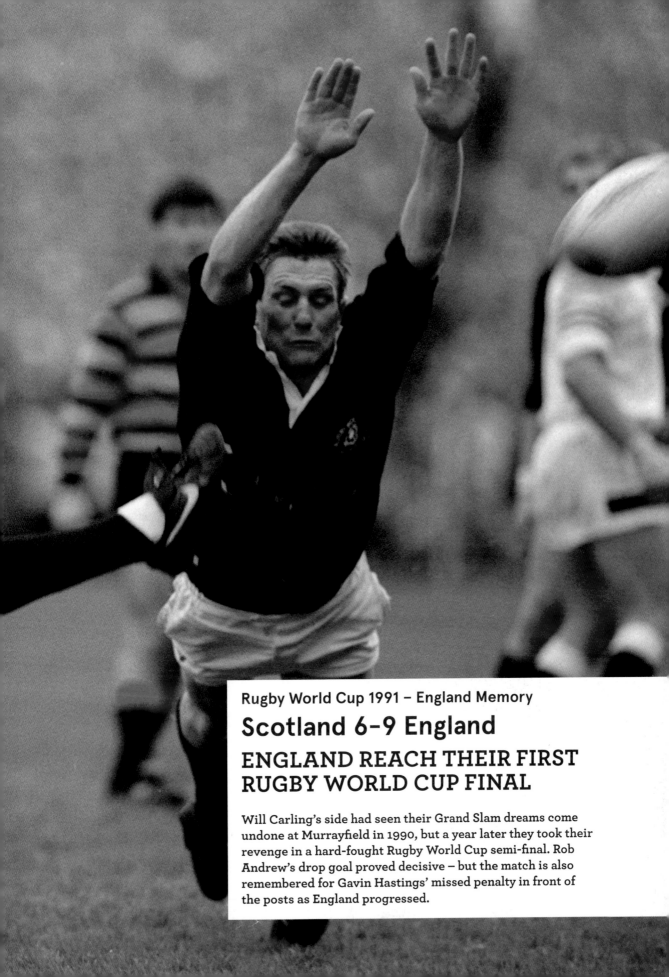

Scotland 6-9 England

ENGLAND REACH THEIR FIRST RUGBY WORLD CUP FINAL

Will Carling's side had seen their Grand Slam dreams come undone at Murrayfield in 1990, but a year later they took their revenge in a hard-fought Rugby World Cup semi-final. Rob Andrew's drop goal proved decisive – but the match is also remembered for Gavin Hastings' missed penalty in front of the posts as England progressed.

The Rugby World Cup Tournament in Numbers

From Jonny Wilkinson's left boot to Grant Fox's most points in a Tournament, look at the records and statistics achieved by players and teams since the creation of Rugby World Cup in 1987.

277

Most points – Jonny Wilkinson

The fly-half is not only England's record points scorer at the Tournament, but he is also the all-time leader. Wilkinson notched up 277 points in 19 matches, including the winning drop goal in 2003.

Most appearances – Jason Leonard

The prop made 22 appearances over four Tournaments for England, more than any other player in the history of the Game. His international career culminated with winning the Tournament in 2003.

22

58

Most penalties kicked – Jonny Wilkinson

Unsurprisingly England's kicking maestro leads the way in penalties kicked at Rugby World Cup for his country, but his tally is also unrivalled by any other player in the world.

19
Youngest try scorer in a Rugby World Cup match – George North

North will be one of the ones to watch at Rugby World Cup 2015, but it was in 2011 that the Welsh winger announced his arrival with two tries against Namibia.

40
Oldest player to appear in a Rugby World Cup match – Diego Ormaechea

During his 20 years of playing for Uruguay the no. 8 made 73 appearances, becoming the oldest player to appear in a Rugby World Cup when he played against South Africa in the 1999 Tournament.

145
Most points by a team in a single match – New Zealand 145–17 Japan, June 4, 1995

New Zealand demolished Japan on their way out of Pool C at Rugby World Cup 1995. They ran in 21 tries, with fly-half Simon Culhane scoring 45 points.

Most drop goals – Jonny Wilkinson

Once again the fly-half holds not only the English record but also the worldwide one, with eight of his 14 drop goals coming during Rugby World Cup 2003.

14

15
Most tries in Rugby World Cup history – Jonah Lomu

Lomu may have only played in Rugby World Cup 1995 and 1999, but the 6ft 5in winger made his mark with 15 tries in just 11 appearances.

Youngest player to win a Rugby World Cup Final – Francois Steyn

The utility back played a pivotal role in South Africa's winning Rugby World Cup 2007 campaign, starting the Final at inside centre and scoring a penalty in the 15–6 win over England

126
Most points scored by a player in one Tournament – Grant Fox, 1987

Fox set the record for the most points scored by a player at the first Rugby World Cup in 1987 and the fly-half's tally of 126 helped guide New Zealand to glory.

Opposite: Such was England fly-half Jonny Wilkinson's impact on the world stage, he holds a number of scoring records, many that will be difficult to beat

Left: Seemingly unstoppable in full flight, New Zealand's Jonah Lomu holds the record of scoring 15 tries in just 11 Rugby World Cup appearances

Rugby World Cup 1991 – England Memory

Australia 12-6 England

AUSTRALIA PIP HOSTS TO TOURNAMENT GLORY

So near, yet so far. In the Final of Rugby World Cup 1991 England attempted to play a more expansive brand of Rugby but were beaten by Australia, who squeezed home despite the best efforts of the likes of Mickey Skinner. Tony Daly's try proved decisive, with England having to wait another 12 years to reach the Final.

Rugby World Cup 2015 Contenders

To be the best you have to beat the best – and the finest unions in world Rugby are heading to England, hoping to stop the hosts from winning their second Rugby World Cup. We profile them here.

New Zealand's Dan Carter takes on the France defence at Rugby World Cup 2011. He remains one of his team's key players

Introduction

From the competitiveness of the Southern Hemisphere to the Northern Hemisphere contenders, we assess the unions looking to triumph in Rugby World Cup 2015.

New Zealand are the favourites, but South Africa beat them in 2014. Ireland are the leading Northern Hemisphere side but have struggled against the Welsh. The French have been in better shape but beat Australia in 2014, while Australia won in Cardiff.

In short, no one knows how Rugby World Cup 2015 is going to unfold, which is the beauty of it all. Excluding England, whose chances are assessed elsewhere, here are the main runners and riders. These are the unions which – with a doff of the cap to Argentina, Italy and the South Sea Islanders – we expect to be in the knockout stages fighting to make it to Twickenham for the Final on October 31.

New Zealand are clearly the favourites, and rightly so. On recent form they lose a Test every two years. Their opponents will take solace from the fact that one defeat is usually enough at a Rugby World Cup, as France have proven against New Zealand on a couple of famous occasions. With Richie McCaw, Dan Carter, Kieran Read, Julian Savea and friends in the form of their lives few would bet against them, but there are other contenders who are quietly confident.

Chief among them will be South Africa, who inflicted New Zealand's most recent defeat. Battle-hardened and streetwise, they will fancy a second Tournament victory in three attempts.

Australia are more of an unknown quantity, rebuilding and replanning after a change of coach during 2014. The talent has always been there. Michael Cheika could well be the man to bring it to the fore.

Moving on to Europe, Ireland look extremely dangerous. Joe Schmidt has proved a superb appointment, and the team is proving there really is life after Brian O'Driscoll.

Then we have Wales, a side capable of brilliance and one that will enjoy the benefit of playing two of their pool matches on home turf at the Millennium Stadium.

France are somewhat more unpredictable, but they are finding talented Test performers at just the right time in Camille Lopez and Teddy Thomas.

So in short, it could be any of them – or it could, of course, be England. No team has ever won the Tournament three times, but New Zealand, South Africa and Australia all have the chance to do so now. Wales, Ireland and France have never won it.

If Stuart Lancaster's men aren't victorious, then something has to give.

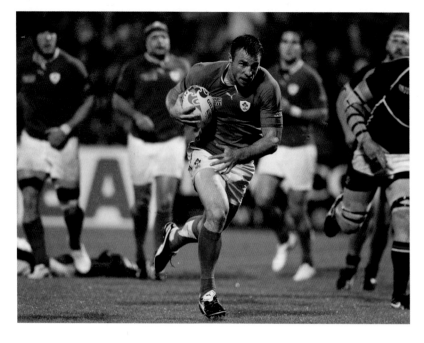

Above: South Africa's Pat Lambie is a highly respected ball handler and proven match winner

Opposite: Players such as Ireland's Tommy Bowe will be relishing the opportunity to test their skills against the very best sides

"We've beaten Australia, we've beaten Wales, we've put 55 points on France ... New Zealand we've beaten before and pushed them close in the summer series. So, absolutely we can win it."

England Head Coach, Stuart Lancaster

Australia

Improving under new coach Michael Cheika, Australia have the experience and Tournament know-how to be a real threat at Rugby World Cup 2015.

Australian Rugby has tended to thrive in adversity and there are clear signs they are moving on from a difficult 2014 and will be a genuine threat at Rugby World Cup 2015.

There can be no doubt they have the players to do so, particularly in a wonderfully talented back division. Will Genia, Nick Phipps, Quade Cooper, Bernard Foley, Matt Toomua, Tevita Kuridrani, Adam Ashley-Cooper, Kurtley Beale and the peerless Israel Folau would push for inclusion in any Test side.

The forward pack has endured a rather more difficult time in recent years, particularly in the scrum, but Michael Hooper, Rob Simmons and

Stephen Moore are among the best in the business.

And despite the perception that 2014 was a poor year for Australia, there are genuine reasons for encouragement as they approach Rugby World Cup 2015. They did not plan on losing Head Coach Ewen McKenzie two days before they left to play in Europe, but in Cheika they were able to appoint the only man to win top-tier Rugby championships in both hemispheres – the Heineken Cup with Leinster in 2009 and Super 15 with the New South Wales Waratahs in 2014.

Certainly, the noises coming out of the Australia camp during November were positive. The new man also unearthed some real gems.

He can now choose between two very different but equally effective half-back pairings, in Phipps–Foley and Genia–Cooper.

Kuridrani has long been thought of as a talented player but he came to the fore in 2014, with Australian great Stirling Mortlock declaring he will be wearing the union's No. 13 shirt for the next decade.

Adam Ashley-Cooper's talent has long been recognised but his importance to team spirit was demonstrated when he turned up for the team photo ahead of his 100th Test in October in full cricket whites, raising his bat to all four corners of the stadium in Brisbane to recognise his century.

Then we have Nick Cummins, aka "The Honey Badger". Fresh from a stint in Japan, this most entertaining and charming of characters has the skill and personality to become the type of star who transcends his sport and becomes a household name.

There is still work to do, and Cheika is well aware of which areas need strengthening, but if his side gets out of a pool that includes England and Wales, then no one will want to face them in the knockout stages.

Left: Kurtley Beale's lightning pace and direct style will be major assets to the Australian team

"For me, you'd never write the Australians off. They always seem to get it right at Rugby World Cup time, they're always very competitive. In general, I think the depth – especially in the backs – is very good."

New Zealand legend, Sean Fitzpatrick

Below: Being placed in the same pool as England and Wales, Australia will have to be ready to perform from the off

France

An unpredictable side capable of anything, France will be hopeful of repeating their performance in 2011, when they reached the Final.

It may be a cliché to say that France are unpredictable, but that doesn't make it any less true.

If you take 2014 as an example, Philippe Saint-André's team put in some fine performances including a five-try victory over Fiji. They then followed this up with a pulsating 29-26 win against Australia in a match that was probably the finest of the Internationals.

But then it all fell apart against Argentina, with the South Americans winning in Paris for the first time since 2007 to ensure that France entered 2015 on a sour note.

Yet this has often been the French way. Just look back at 2011; defeated by Tonga in one of the biggest shocks in Rugby World Cup history, they hauled themselves into the Final. Indeed, many observers felt they were

better than New Zealand on the day and could have returned home with the Webb Ellis Cup for the first time.

And recent form means we do not know what to expect from a French side in a pool dominated by countries within the Six Nations. They appear alongside Ireland, Italy, Romania and Canada.

In the likes of Wesley Fofana, Gaël Fickou, Noa Nakaitaci and Yoann

> "I have confidence in our players. They have the quality and the desire to win Rugby World Cup 2015."

France Head Coach, Philippe Saint-André

Huget, France clearly have the type of attacking talent that could make a real impact at Rugby World Cup 2015.

There is enough brawn and brain in the pack to upset the best too. Thierry Dusautoir is an inspirational leader, while old heads Nicolas Mas and Pascal Papé will relish one last shot at glory after marking 23 years worth of international service between them.

And in Saint-André they have one of the most intriguing coaches in the competition. Winner of 69 caps for his country in a glorious playing career, he captained the French side in 34 Tests, winning 25 of them.

Known as one of the most inventive players of his generation, Saint-André built a France side that was considered by some to be lacking in invention, particularly when they finished bottom of the Six Nations in 2013.

But three wins from five the following year, allied to the displays against Australia and Fiji, means there is now some optimism.

In truth, though, we have little idea what to expect from this talented side.

Opposite: Despite being beaten Finalists in Rugby World Cup 2011, France have not performed to a consistent high standard since

Right: With determined players such as Nicolas Mas, France can never be underestimated

Ireland

A side transformed under new coach Joe Schmidt goes into the Tournament with genuine aspirations of winning their first Rugby World Cup.

If Joe Schmidt's stock was not high enough already, his actions on November 22, 2014 raised his status to new, uncharted territory. That day was spent masterminding an Ireland victory over Australia to ensure a clean sweep in Ireland's Autumn Internationals, the first time they had won all their matches in November since 2006.

A breathless first half had ended 20–20, and Schmidt's calm half-time command to slow the pace had proved decisive, as Ireland won by six points. Then, having conducted his post-match duties, Schmidt calmly checked himself in to hospital to have his appendix removed.

An Ireland spokesman admitted their coach had been "in agony" throughout the day, while assistant coach Les Kiss laughingly admitted Schmidt had "toughed the day out" in typically understated fashion.

And after a day like that, is it any wonder Ireland's players will run through brick walls for their leader?

Schmidt has had a stunning impact since succeeding Declan Kidney in 2013, leading Ireland to the 2014 Six Nations title in what was a fitting farewell to Brian O'Driscoll as they won in Paris for the first time since 2000. A year later he followed up that success with another title, the first time Ireland has won back-to-back titles since 1949.

With Paul O'Connell, Jamie Heaslip, Rory Best and Cian Healy powering the pack, former Leinster Head Coach Schmidt has plenty to work with up front. But the backs are coming together nicely too. Conor Murray and Johnny Sexton are one of the finest half-back combinations in the world, while Tommy Bowe, Simon Zebo and Rob Kearney form a fine back-three combination.

With Robbie Henshaw demonstrating he may be ready to step into O'Driscoll's shoes, it is not hard to see that Schmidt is building a side without too many weaknesses.

Drawn in a pool with France, Italy, Romania and Canada, Ireland will fancy their chances of being genuine dark horses at Rugby World Cup 2015.

Ireland may be peaking at just the right time.

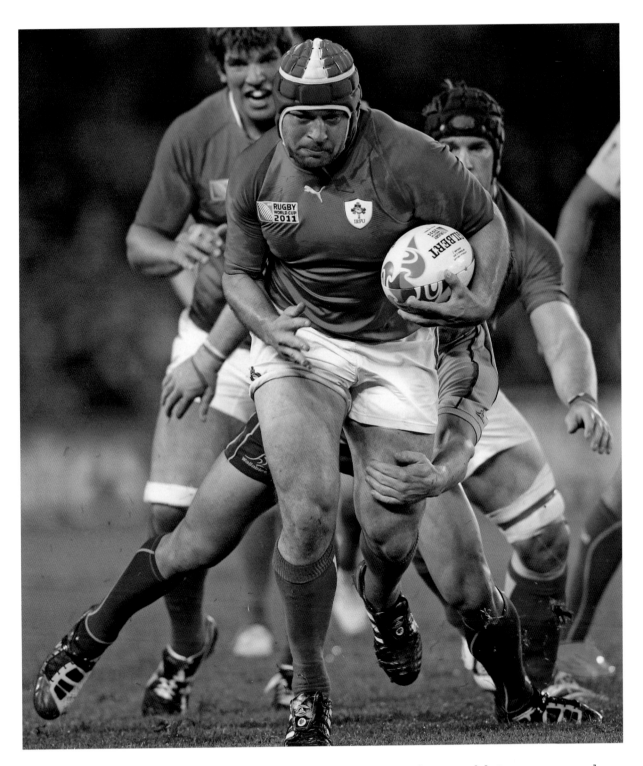

Above: Ireland hooker Rory Best's experience will be invaluable to Ireland

Opposite: Ireland's Johnny Sexton is a prolific goal kicker and makes an essential contribution to the team's firepower

"For Ireland to win a Rugby World Cup you need a load of things to go your way ... But Ireland certainly have a chance of winning Rugby World Cup 2015. You don't go out and play unless you believe that."

Ireland Captain, Paul O'Connell

New Zealand

The reigning World Champions, the best side on the planet and the ones to beat – Richie McCaw and company are desperate to retain their crown.

Two-time Rugby World Cup winners New Zealand have been one of world Rugby's strongest performers since they lifted the Trophy in 2011

Sometimes, mere statistics aren't enough. It is simple to say that New Zealand lost just one of the 28 matches they played during 2013 and 2014, but it doesn't quite demonstrate the extent to which they have dominated world Rugby over the past few years.

Winning Rugby World Cup 2011 on home soil eased the pressure slightly on battle-hardened players such as Richie McCaw and Kieran Read, and they have responded by hitting new heights.

Their loss at Twickenham Stadium in the autumn of 2012, allied to a 27–25 defeat in Johannesburg two years later, has given the rest of the world some hope. New Zealand can have off days, they can be beaten.

The problem is that even their off days are usually better than the rest. Take the tour of Europe in autumn 2014. Going into the tour, New Zealand were concerned they were finishing matches poorly. After putting in brutal, match-winning late efforts to beat England, Scotland and Wales, the concern switched to whether they were starting matches well enough. Identify a problem, fix it and move on is their motto under Steve Hansen. And the theme under Hansen, the former assistant who succeeded Graham Henry following that victory in 2011,

has been one of improvement and weeding out the small errors.

The old stagers – McCaw, Read, Keven Mealamu and Dan Carter – are all still very much part of the side and will look to become the first men to successfully defend their Rugby World Cup crown.

But the new generation have established themselves too, and they seem ready to continue this astonishing run of success.

Brodie Retallick made his New Zealand debut only in 2012, but two years later he was named World Rugby Player of the Year after forming a superb second-row partnership with Sam Whitelock, a player who will himself turn just 27 during the Tournament.

Julian Savea is another who was blooded by Hansen during 2012, but he is widely recognised as the finest finisher in world Rugby. There can be no higher praise than that given by Hansen during 2014, when he said: "I think Julian is probably better (than Jonah Lomu). Jonah was a great player, but I think Julian has got more to his game to be honest and that's saying something."

It certainly is, and Savea's record of 30 tries in 33 Tests compares favourably to Lomu's record of 37 in 63 Tests.

New Zealand will be the team to beat and are major contenders to win Rugby World Cup 2015.

Players such as Kieran Read (above) and Richie McCaw provide the New Zealand team with big-match experience, while the likes of Julian Savea have the capacity to unlock opposition defences and change matches

South Africa

The only side to beat New Zealand in either 2013 or 2014, South Africa are tipped by many to become the first side to win the Tournament on three occasions.

The team South Africa boss Heyneke Meyer will name for his union's Rugby World Cup opener against Japan will ooze class and experience. He can call on over half of the side that won the 2007 Tournament, with a new and exciting generation of players coming through to replace them. From Bryan Habana to JP Pietersen on the wings and Victor Matfield returning in the second row, this is a team that knows exactly what it is doing.

Their quarter-final defeat to Australia four years ago remains a source of great pain and inspiration. Revenge would be sweet.

They are boosted by the return of the inspirational Matfield, returning to the international fold after a three-year absence and looking like he has never been away. He may no longer have old partner in crime Bakkies Botha alongside him, but the young tyro Eben Etzebeth more than makes up for that. Lock is a position of huge strength for South Africa.

As you'd expect, they are strong up front too. Adriaan Strauss would start at hooker for most sides but is likely to play second fiddle to the wonderful Bismarck du Plessis, while Jannie du Plessis, Coenie

Oosthuizen and the man they call "The Beast", Tendai Mtawarira, are superb props.

Duane Vermeulen is one of the world's premier No. 8s, but the real boost for Meyer during 2014 was the development of some young talents.

Pat Lambie's skill has been known about for some time, and the manner in which he steered his side past England at Twickenham in November was hugely impressive. But Handré Pollard, who will be just 21 when the Tournament takes place, appears to be a potential superstar. His two tries in the win over New Zealand in October (which was sealed by a Lambie penalty) announced the arrival of a top-drawer star. Expect him to be at the heart of South Africa's challenge for the next decade.

There was a huge blow in the form of the knee injury suffered by captain Jean De Villier, which renders his participation in the Tournament very doubtful, but Willie le Roux's performances at full-back earned him a nomination for World Rugby Player of the Year.

With strength in depth and an experienced coach, South Africa will be genuine contenders.

Above: South Africa's early exit in Rugby World Cup 2011 was difficult to take for this proud Rugby Union. They will be looking to make amends and a record third Rugby World Cup win in 2015

Opposite: South Africa's JP Pietersen has played over 50 times for his country and this year's Tournament will be his third Rugby World Cup

Wales

Boasting the Lions Head Coach and captain in their ranks, Wales are going to be a force to be reckoned with in this Rugby World Cup.

There are few cannier operators than Warren Gatland, and few more dangerous sides than the Welsh team he will send into battle in Rugby World Cup 2015.

It is odd to think that Gatland's first coaching job was with Galwegians in Ireland but his career has progressed rapidly since, taking in spells with Thames Valley, Connacht, Ireland, London Wasps, Waikato, the Lions and now eight years in charge of Wales.

A former hooker who chooses the words he utters in public very carefully, Gatland has guided Wales through a series of off-field political issues with some skill and now has a wonderful squad to choose from.

He is aided by some hugely experienced coaches, in Rob Howley, Shaun Edwards and Robin McBryde. Together they have formed a tight unit, and they are fortunate to have a superb on-field leader in Sam Warburton.

The Lions skipper has grown in stature since bursting into the public consciousness with his displays during Rugby World Cup 2011, where he was one of the players of the Tournament until receiving a red card in the semi-final defeat to France.

Respected across the Game, he is supported in the pack by the likes of Alun Wyn Jones, Richard Hibbard, Bradley Davies and Gethin Jenkins.

Gatland's options in the back row are superb too, with Dan Lydiate, Justin Tipuric and Taulupe Faletau among those looking to line up alongside Warburton.

The development of Rhys Webb to challenge Mike Phillips at scrum-half has been a welcome boost, while Jamie Roberts is a commanding and highly respected centre.

The back three reeks of class too. George North is a one-man wrecking ball and Alex Cuthbert a deadly finisher, while Leigh Halfpenny's goal kicking and all-round performances from full-back were such a stunning feature of the Lions tour.

Gatland will want more consistency from his side as they approach the "Pool of Death" alongside Australia, England, Fiji and Uruguay.

In the summer of 2014 they lost narrowly to South Africa before claiming revenge at home in November – but only after losing to New Zealand and Australia

In the 2015 Six Nations, they recovered from a defeat to England in the opening match to finish with four wins out of five, including victory over eventual champions Ireland.

So in short, expect more "Warren-ball" – that fast, physical brand of rugby which has worked so well – and a brutal challenge put up by a powerful and passionate Welsh side. Time will tell how far it can take them.

Wales will be tough competitors at Rugby World Cup 2015 and they will be determined to progress

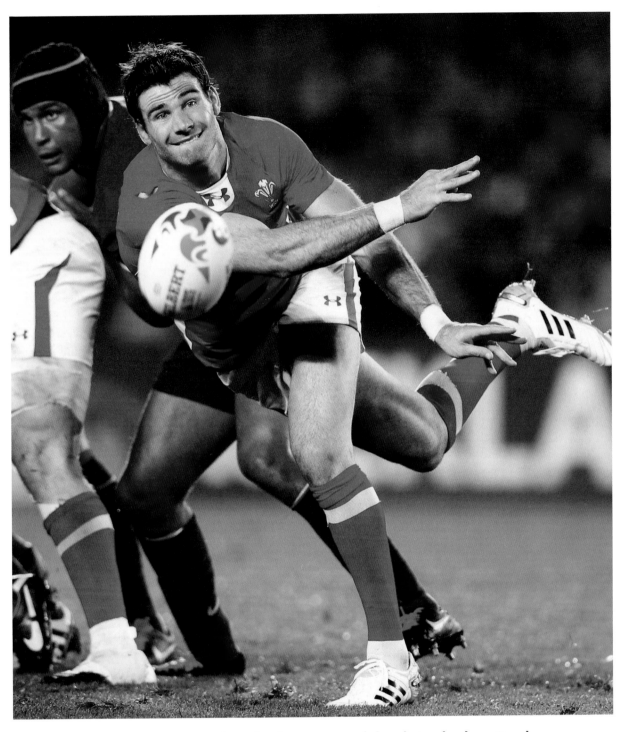

"We had a group of death in the last Rugby World Cup so we are used to the situation. It's a fascinating pool. ... As for England v Wales, there is enough rivalry there without it being a Rugby World Cup."

Wales Captain, Sam Warburton

Above: Wales play a fast, physical brand of Rugby and they have become one of the strongest Northern Hemisphere teams

Rugby World Cup 1995 – England Memory

England 25–22 Australia

ANDREW'S DROP GOAL SEALS QUARTER-FINAL WIN

Another England fly-half would seal his place in history with a drop goal against Australia, but it was Rob Andrew who was the hero in the quarter-final of Rugby World Cup 1995 in Cape Town. Andrew's effort was technically superb, bisecting the posts from wide out on the left to send England into the semi-finals and spark wild scenes of celebration.

England at Rugby World Cup in Quotes

Whether in triumph or defeat, these quotes, from England's players and coaching staff, tell the story of the team's Tournament experiences.

"I have never seen a game with five drop goals. We tried everything, but it was not to be. The game is over, Rugby World Cup is over for England. That's it."

Sir Clive Woodward after the quarter-final of Rugby World Cup 1999

"We came very close to blowing it. Every decision seemed to go against them, and yet they still won, and that is the sign of a champion team."

Sir Clive Woodward after the Final of Rugby World Cup 2003

"Winning Rugby World Cup was not about doing one thing one hundred per cent better, but about doing one hundred things one per cent better."

Sir Clive Woodward

"I did have a couple of beers, but that was only really as a solidarity thing with the other guys. There are times for letting yourself go, but Saturday night I just wanted to let it all soak in."

Jonny Wilkinson after Rugby World Cup 2003

"I can't say enough about the team, because we had the lead and we lost it but we came back. And I can't say enough about Wilko at the end. He is a very special player, a very special person."

Martin Johnson after the Final of Rugby World Cup 2003

"I don't think it's sunk in for anyone yet. It's been more a case of winning a match and then going out on a Saturday night with mates."

Jason Leonard after the Final of Rugby World Cup 2003

Captain Martin Johnson holds aloft the Webb Ellis Cup in 2003 – the greatest moment for England in Rugby World Cup history to date

"We gave ourselves a massive task, but I'm proud of the way the boys took on that task. This team will stay together, keeping building, and I'm sure the next Rugby World Cup will be different."

Jonny Wilkinson following the quarter-final of Rugby World Cup 2011

"Just holding the Webb Ellis Cup was a buzz, although I have to say it's pretty small. For all the effort we've put in, you'd think they'd have given Martin Johnson something bigger."

Lewis Moody after the Final of Rugby World Cup 2003

"We've had a magical time. Fair play to South Africa. They were the better team and this is their victory. We have to wait for four years so they'd better enjoy it."

Phil Vickery following the Final of Rugby World Cup 2007

"It might be difficult to understand but I never felt we were going to lose that game – it was the inner steel, the inner belief within the squad that whatever it takes we will win."

Lawrence Dallaglio following the Final of Rugby World Cup 2003

New Zealand 45–29 England
LOMU MAGIC JUST TOO GOOD

Rugby has never seen a player as destructive and powerful as Jonah Lomu and England simply had no answer to his brilliance in the semi-final of Rugby World Cup 1995. The New Zealand wing scored four breathtaking tries as his union advanced to the Final despite England registering four tries of their own in a stunning match.

England
Rugby

England's Main Men

Stuart Lancaster has made his choice and put his faith in the players he hopes will guide England to Rugby World Cup glory. Here we profile 20 of the key men to wear the Red Rose in Rugby World Cup 2015.

In passionate voice, England sing the national anthem prior to a game against Scotland at Twickenham Stadium in 2015

Introduction

England Rugby

The pressure of a home Rugby World Cup is immense, but these are the men the entire nation hopes will lead England to glory on October 31.

"Very few ever get the chance in rugby terms to get to Everest, the top of Everest. You have the chance." So said Jim Telfer. It is unlikely that the proud Scot would want his own words spurring on an England side, but for the men Stuart Lancaster has chosen to represent their country at a home Rugby World Cup, this really is their Everest.

Telfer was referring to the Lions and their tour of South Africa in 1997, but for an Englishman the thought of lifting the Webb Ellis Cup on home soil is as good as it gets.

Stuart Lancaster has had much of the squad he will entrust with that awesome responsibility inked in for some time. Chris Robshaw, Owen Farrell, Ben Youngs, Dan Cole and Alex Corbisiero all started in Lancaster's first match in charge at Murrayfield and have been ever-present since then. The Head Coach also made it clear that Courtney Lawes and Joe Launchbury would be in his squad if fit.

The challenge has been to transform these fine young talents into seasoned internationals. The only way to do that was playing matches, which is why Lancaster has been consistent in the majority of his team selections.

Farrell could have almost 40 caps by the time England open Rugby World Cup 2015 against Fiji, while by the end of 2014 Robshaw had captained his country on more occasions than anyone bar Will Carling and Martin Johnson.

The process of blooding new talent to pair with swiftly established names has continued. Over the course of 2014 Jonny May, Jack Nowell, and Anthony Watson were among those given their chance at the highest level.

Then there was the case of George Ford, a youngster who has started to make good on his stunning promise. The former Leicester Tigers player is now guiding an impressive Bath side, and his battle with Farrell for the England no. 10 shirt will be fascinating. Friends since school, they have a healthy rivalry that will be vital for Lancaster.

These, then, are the men Lancaster and the country will make huge demands on over the next few weeks and months. Here we look at their backgrounds, their history and what they have achieved.

Then we shall wait and see if they will climb their very own Everest.

England will go head to head with Australia in 2015. Their last encounter in 2003 will live long in the memory of all England fans

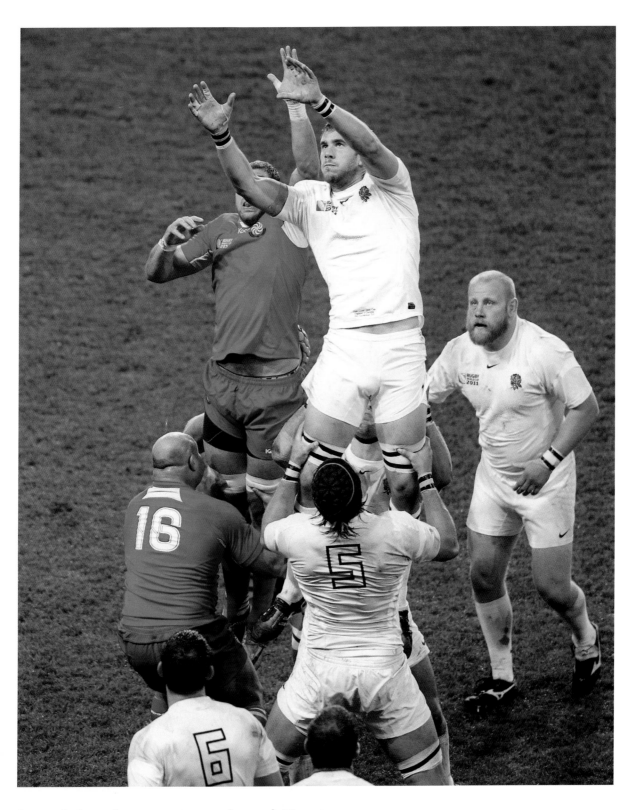

"It is definitely a pretty tough pool. To win a Rugby World Cup you have to win big games."

England Head Coach, Stuart Lancaster

Above: The England team will be determined to win Rugby World Cup 2015 on home soil

Alex Corbisiero

England Rugby

England's "hip-hop prop" has enjoyed a stunning rise to fame and played in both the Lions' victorious Tests in the 2013 tour of Australia.

Alex Corbisiero proved his mettle against Martin Castrogiovanni on his England debut against Italy in February 2011, but it was events after the match which demonstrated to his team-mates that he was going to be a regular on the international stage.

Until then Corbisiero had kept quiet about his musical talents, but when it came to his turn to sing an initiation song on the team bus he did not hold back, rapping about the match, his team-mates, what it meant to win and to wear the England shirt. It is a theme he has continued since.

He was a member of Martin Johnson's squad for Rugby World Cup 2011 and really kicked on in the following year's Six Nations under Stuart Lancaster, a coach who has never needed convincing of the prop's talents.

After he impressed in the win over New Zealand, a knee injury ruled him out of the Six Nations in 2013 and seemed certain to finish his Lions dream. But Corbisiero recovered swiftly and, after again impressing on England's summer tour of Argentina, he was called up for the Lions. He went on to play in both of their victories over Australia, scoring the first try in the decisive Third Test and helping to demolish the Australia scrum.

Injuries disrupted Corbisiero's 2014, but he is expected to be a key part of the England squad.

England appearances: 19
England points: 0

Dan Cole

England
Rugby

Jokingly referred to by some as Henry VIII due to his resemblance to the famous king, Dan Cole is Rugby Royalty.

The esteem in which Dan Cole is held was perhaps best demonstrated by the horror that greeted the news that he had suffered a serious neck injury in February 2014.

In his own quiet, understated manner Cole has become perhaps the most important member of the England side. He had missed just one of England's previous 45 Tests, developing from a talented youngster into a genuinely world-class prop.

"When names like that come back on the team sheet, it gives you confidence and puts a bit of fear into the opposition," said Leicester Tigers boss Richard Cockerill on Cole's return from his neck problem, and Stuart Lancaster would surely have uttered similar sentiments.

David Wilson has proved a more than adequate replacement but Cole's set-piece brilliance, allied to his speed and fitness in the loose, have seen him hailed as one of England's finest ever props. Indeed, his ability to win turnovers, as well as speed of thought and hand, make him a key part of England's counter-attacking game – a feat few props are able to claim.

A vital member of England's 2011 Six Nations winning side and the 2013 Lions tour party, England will be hoping that Cole is crowned king in London – just as Henry VIII was more than 500 years ago.

England appearances: **50**
England points: **5**

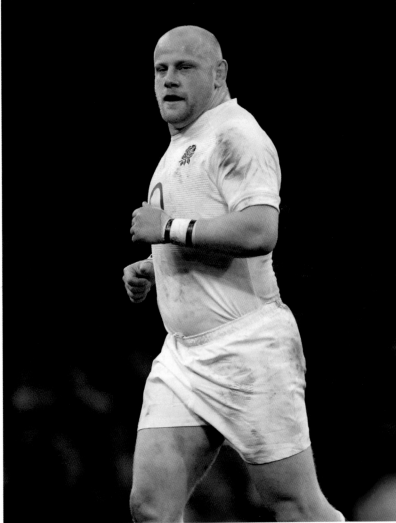

James Haskell

England Rugby

A physical and versatile back row forward, James Haskell is now one of England's senior players.

James Haskell's England career has gone through three distinct phases. Back in 2007 he was the young pup, the Wasps flanker who played and learnt alongside the great Lawrence Dallaglio and was tipped to have just as big an influence.

Then there was the traveller, the man who played his club rugby in France, Japan and New Zealand but continued to knock on the international door, playing in Rugby World Cup 2011.

Finally we have the elder statesman, the most experienced player in Stuart Lancaster's setup. Haskell is home now, captaining Wasps, and taking those leadership skills into camp with England.

His aggressive approach and rampaging style are vital to England, and it seems Haskell is developing into the player many thought he would become when he won the Heineken Cup in 2007.

Haskell had already made his England debut in Cardiff by this point, but he missed out on selection for Rugby World Cup 2007.

Haskell scored a brace of tries against the Welsh in 2010 and played in five matches at Rugby World Cup 2011.

In 2013, he completed a half century of Test appearances by playing against Wales in Cardiff, and is now the most capped player in England's Rugby World Cup 2015 squad.

England appearances: 58
England points: 20

Tom Youngs

The third member of his family to play for England, Youngs has developed into a top-class hooker who featured heavily for the Lions in 2013.

England Rugby

The conversation that transformed Tom Youngs' career took place in 2009. The 22-year-old centre had just captained the Leicester second team against Saracens, a match which featured an old-fashioned dust-up with an opposition prop. Heyneke Meyer, then the Leicester Tigers coach and now in charge of South Africa, approached Youngs and made a radical suggestion.

"He came up to me and said, 'I think you've got what it takes to play in the front row. I want to make you a hooker'," Youngs recalled three years later, as he prepared to make his international debut in his new position.

Certainly, Youngs' career has gone from strength to strength. From being a player struggling to cement a position in the Leicester side, he is now an England squad regular and a Lion.

Unsurprisingly considering his former position, his mobility and direct running style make him more versatile than others who wear the no. 2 shirt, while he has added to a proud family tradition; father Nick and brother Ben were already internationals by the time he made his debut against Fiji in November 2012.

Within eight months he had played in all three of the Lions' Tests in Australia before returning to action with England. Injury curtailed his 2014 season, but big things are expected in 2015.

England appearances: 22
England points: 0

Joe Marler

If you play with a bleached mohawk, you had better be good – and thankfully for the unmissable Joe Marler, he really is.

England appearances: 31
England points: 0

To begin with, all anybody could talk about was Joe Marler's hair, and then his beard. Now, they talk about superb scrummaging technique, brutal tackling ability and his rampaging running style.

A very modern-day prop, Marler enjoyed a stunning 2014, developing from talented youngster into a top-drawer player, coming up against and beating the very best in the business. His growing maturity and leadership abilities were recognised when he was appointed Harlequins captain, and he has become a genuine force to be reckoned with.

A real character and well liked within the squad, Marler was first called into the England training camp in 2010 but did not make his debut until two years later, against South Africa.

He featured in all five matches during the Six Nations in 2013, but it was in 2014 that he really came into his own, starting 11 matches for his country. The one championship match he missed was the trip to Italy, but he had a good reason because his partner went into labour shortly before the match, meaning Marler joined the growing band of fathers within the England squad.

He is still extremely young for a top-class prop, so we should expect to see Marler – and both his hair and beard – on the international stage for many years to come.

Dave Attwood

England Rugby

A physics graduate who made the grade with England in 2014, Dave Attwood brings a competitive edge to the second-row battle.

Dave Attwood will never forget the week leading up to England's Test against New Zealand in November 2014. Told by Stuart Lancaster he would be starting the match, the Bath lock admitted he felt that he was making his debut all over again, for this was a second coming in international Rugby some four years after he first played for his country.

There was just one problem: his fiancée, Bridget, was due to give birth and he might have to miss the match. Attwood agonised over what to do, but thankfully little Jessica was born on the Tuesday ahead of the match and her father went on to play superbly against New Zealand.

It was the culmination of three years of hard graft since Attwood switched Gloucester for Bath in a bid to restart his international career.

His lineout prowess and athleticism had seen him picked as a replacement for each match in the Six Nations of 2014, but it was in November of that year that he cemented his place in the squad, taking his chance superbly in the absence of the injured Joe Launchbury.

He started each of the four Tests and was one of England's most impressive players, which he said at the time had something to do with "Dad-strength" – the new arrival giving him an extra incentive to perform and make his family proud. So far it has worked well for England.

England appearances: 20
England points: 0

Joe Launchbury

England Rugby

A youngster who performs like a seasoned veteran, Joe Launchbury has made the transition from club to Test Rugby seem almost absurdly easy.

Twickenham Stadium, February 22, 2014: with under 90 seconds left on the clock, England lead Ireland 13–10 after a titanic tussle. Ireland break quickly, the ball shipped out by Gordon D'Arcy and Brian O'Driscoll to Dave Kearney. The wing cuts inside to draw in England full-back Mike Brown, knowing D'Arcy is inside him and will have a clear run to the line. But as Kearney starts to do so a figure in white throws himself at him, Joe Launchbury stretching every last inch of his frame to make a stunning tap-tackle.

It summed up his international career to date. Locks aren't supposed to cover 60m in a matter of seconds to make a match-winning tap-tackle on a wing in the dying moments of a match. Then again, you're not supposed to adapt to top-level rugby so swiftly.

Wasps lock Launchbury was just 21 when he was first called up by England, and is now a mainstay of the pack and one of the most exciting young forwards in the world. Equally comfortable in the back row, he has gone head-to-head with the likes of Paul O'Connell and come out on top. His progress has been recognised; he was named England Player of the Year in the 2012/13 season, his first in international Rugby.

Few would bet against Launchbury becoming an all-time England great.

England appearances: 22
England points: 10

Courtney Lawes

A force of nature who can change the course of a match with one big hit, Courtney Lawes is one of England's enforcers and most important forwards.

England appearances: 38
England points: 0

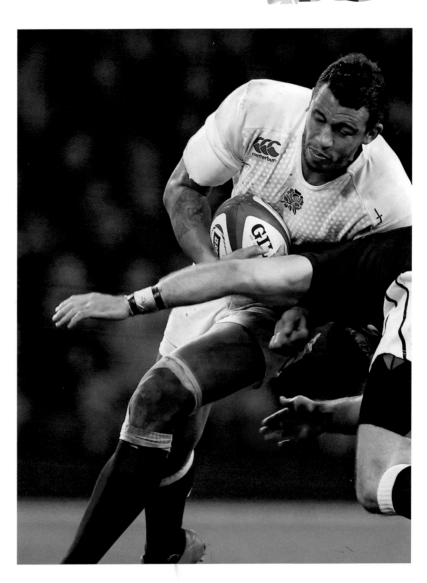

It says it all that Rugby World Cup 2003-winning second row Ben Kay has described Courtney Lawes as "a world-class player and one of the best defensive locks I have seen in a long time".

High praise indeed, but Lawes certainly deserves it. Now a mainstay of the England team, he and Launchbury could genuinely claim to be the best second-row combination in the world, and they both have plenty of rugby left ahead of them.

Known initially for his huge hits – an attribute that is still a major feature of his game as France fly-half Jules Plisson will attest – he has developed into a genuine all-rounder, as evidenced by the fact he is now England's lineout leader. "He's thrived on that extra responsibility and is asking for more," said England assistant coach Graham Rowntree. "The thing is that it doesn't take away from the rest of his game. He's still playing dynamically, he's tackling well and his breakdown skills are second to none."

Tipped for stardom from an early age, he was first brought into the squad by Martin Johnson but has thrived under Lancaster and Jim Mallinder at Northampton Saints. An automatic first-choice since late 2013, he is fulfilling his considerable potential and will be vital to England's chances for success.

Chris Robshaw

England
Rugby

England captain and the heartbeat of the side, Chris Robshaw has developed into a world-class flanker who has made the no. 7 shirt his own.

When Stuart Lancaster was appointed England's interim Head Coach in 2012 one of his first tasks was to appoint a new captain. Eyebrows were raised when he decided on Chris Robshaw, the Harlequins flanker who at that stage had just one cap and 53 minutes of world Rugby to his name.

It proved to be an inspired choice. Robshaw is now the heartbeat of the side, the on-field personification of everything Lancaster is looking for: pride, work-rate, discipline and character. That he is a breakdown specialist and one of the finest tacklers in world Rugby is a rather handy bonus, and few can doubt that Robshaw has grown into the role during Lancaster's time in charge.

Twice named Premiership Player of the Year, Robshaw is the public face of the England team and his consistency is demonstrated by the fact that by the end of 2014 he had enjoyed more matches as England captain than anyone bar Will Carling and Martin Johnson.

Perhaps his finest moment came in the win against New Zealand in November 2012, when he put personal criticism behind him to outplay the legendary Richie McCaw, although his display in the win against Australia two years later was also outstanding.

England will see more of the same in 2015. England's leader can carry them home.

England appearances: 37
England points: 10

Tom Wood

England Rugby

An abrasive, ball-carrying back row who has thrived under Stuart Lancaster, Tom Wood has excelled on the flank leading into the Tournament.

England appearances: **36**
England points: **0**

Is there a more intimidating place to make your England debut than Cardiff on a Friday night? Probably not, and it was a sign of Tom Wood's character that Martin Johnson felt entirely comfortable handing the Northampton Saints back row his first international start in the bear-pit of the Millennium Stadium in 2011.

He needn't have worried: Wood put in a stunning display, making 48m with the ball in hand and contributing 13 tackles as England surged to victory. When fit he has scarcely left the side – or let his standards drop – since.

One of the most inspirational speakers in the England side, Wood played in all five matches during that season's victorious Six Nations and was touted for the captaincy when Stuart Lancaster succeeded Johnson after Rugby World Cup 2011.

Lancaster chose Chris Robshaw instead but has made Wood a central member of the team's leadership group, as evidenced by the fact he captained the side in Robshaw's absence during the tour of South America in 2013.

A central member of the side since then, he started all of England's key matches in 2014, having shown great fortitude to come back from a serious foot injury.

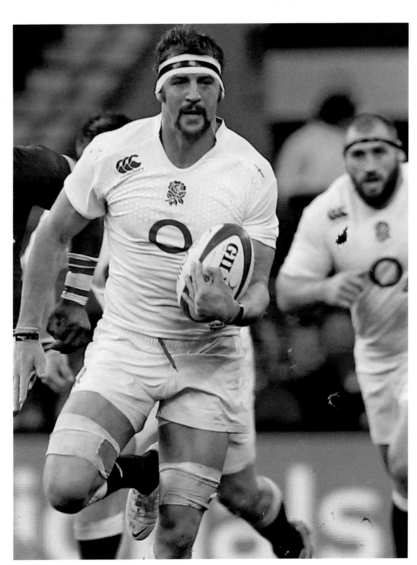

Billy Vunipola

England Rugby

A powerful No. 8 whose direct running makes him a real threat, Billy Vunipola enjoyed a superb 2014 to emerge as an international-class forward.

England appearances: 17
England points: 15

The last thing Argentina's defenders wanted was to see Billy Vunipola running at them. Though the match in Salta was all but over, Vunipola wanted to make an impression on his international debut in 2013. His brother, Mako, was playing for the Lions in Australia and he was keen to show Stuart Lancaster what he could do in South America. He broke off the back of a scrum and stormed over for a try on his debut. No one has been able to hold him back since.

Vunipola is part of a proud Tongan rugby dynasty with his father, grandfather and six uncles playing internationally. His upbringing in Bristol and then a spell at Harrow School were crucial to his development.

He broke through at Wasps before moving to Saracens to play alongside his brother, while his first international start came against Australia at Twickenham Stadium in November 2013 – a match in which he performed superbly.

He cemented his place after that, and was singled out for particular praise for his role in the 2015 campaign. "What a series, what a man, outstanding," said Andy Farrell of the No.8.

His battle with Ben Morgan ahead of and during Rugby World Cup 2015 should be utterly fascinating, particularly as Vunipola hasn't taken a single backwards step since Salta.

Ben Morgan

A qualified plumber who used to work on a building site, Ben Morgan came to Rugby late but is now an England regular.

England appearances: **27**
England points: **25**

Some players are fast-tracked through Academies to the international stage or thought of as future superstars well before they step inside the Twickenham Stadium dressing room. Not Ben Morgan. Instead, the No.8 was working on a building site and playing amateur rugby for Merthyr Tydfil.

Then the Scarlets saw his potential and gave Morgan a chance. He lost 19kg in weight and began to attract attention from all quarters, with Martin Johnson and Wales boss Warren Gatland both asking him to represent their country.

Morgan chose England and moved to Gloucester, being rewarded with an international debut under Stuart Lancaster at Murrayfield in 2012.

Since then Morgan has enjoyed a ding-dong battle with Billy Vunipola for the No.8 shirt, but he hit new heights in the 2014. Named as a replacement against New Zealand and South Africa, he scored against the latter before being restored to the starting XV for the matches against Samoa and Australia.

He rewarded Lancaster for his show of faith, scoring England's two tries in the 26–17 victory over Australia.

A broken leg kept him out of the England team in 2015, but he is hoping to recover in time to challenge Vunipola for a starting position in the squad this September.

Danny Care

England Rugby ®

In November 2014 Care won his 50th cap for his country and this quick-thinking, dynamic scrum-half has become a key squad member.

When Stuart Lancaster first came across Danny Care in the Yorkshire Under-16 side, few would have imagined that a decade later they would be working together on the international stage.

A pacy, creative scrum-half, Care brought up a half-century of caps for his country against South Africa in November 2014, some six years after making his debut against New Zealand in Auckland.

Lancaster has played a vital role in Care's development since they first worked together with the Yorkshire age-group side in 2002, with the young scrum-half at that time already progressing rapidly through the Leeds youth system.

Care was then fast-tracked into the Leeds first team, understudying the great Justin Marshall before heading south to join Harlequins.

His development continued apace and he has been locked in battle for the England scrum-half shirt with Ben Youngs since the 2010/11 season.

Now a father and a member of England's leadership group, Care started every one of England's key 2014 fixtures, including their narrow defeat to New Zealand. He then brought up that half-century against South Africa before Youngs played in the final two matches of the year.

A regular contributor of both tries and drop goals to the cause, Care will hope to hit new heights in 2015.

England appearances: 52
England points: 44

78

Ben Youngs

The Leicester player has been an England squad regular since 2010 and has repeatedly shown the quick thinking that will be vital in 2015.

England Rugby

Ben Youngs was a prodigious young talent who immediately made good on his astonishing potential. In just his second Twickenham Stadium start in November 2010 he played a vital role in what may well be the finest-ever try scored there. Few scrum-halves would have gathered a turnover ball on their own line and dummied Australian fly-half Quade Cooper, as Youngs did, before allowing Courtney Lawes to set up Chris Ashton for a thrilling score.

Indeed, he has always enjoyed playing against Australia – something which may come in handy considering they are in England's Rugby World Cup 2015 Pool.

Youngs impressed during Rugby World Cup 2011, scoring two tries, and there was another milestone reached the following year when he started a Twickenham Test alongside brother Tom for the first time when South Africa visited south-west London.

Since then he has enjoyed a battle for the shirt with Danny Care, Richard Wigglesworth and Lee Dickson. It is one that saw Care have the upper hand for much of 2014, but Youngs outstripped him towards the end of the year, performing impressively in the wins against Samoa and Australia. Now we need to see whether he can produce more Twickenham fireworks. Youngs claimed the England shirt in 2015 and will hope to retain it this Autumn.

England appearances: 47
England points: 45

Owen Farrell

England Rugby

As tough as they come and with ice coursing through his veins, Owen Farrell will be vital to England's Rugby World Cup 2015 hopes.

So central has Owen Farrell become to everything about the current England set up that it comes as something of a shock to realise that he made his debut only in February 2012.

A ruthless goal kicker who thinks nothing of tackling a rampaging second row, he will be crucial to Stuart Lancaster's Rugby World Cup 2015 plans.

Son of England backs coach Andy Farrell, he was born in Wigan but became the youngest player to appear in English professional rugby when he made his debut for Saracens aged 17. His international debut followed, but it was against Ireland in 2012 where he really came of age, kicking 20 points as he rammed home England's dominance in the scrum.

His first try came against Australia in November 2013 and highlighted Farrell's eye for a gap and turn of pace, as well as his fabled tactical kicking ability.

He is now a British & Irish Lion and his battle with old schoolmate George Ford for the coveted no. 10 shirt will be fascinating. Farrell can also play at inside centre and England will rely on this competitive, ambitious player as they look to quell the best that the rest of the world has to offer on home soil.

England appearances: **29**
England points: **290**

George Ford

England Rugby

The boy wonder is well on the way to becoming one of England's main men. A prodigious talent, he has every chance of shocking the world in 2015.

The first Englishman to be named IRB Junior Player of the Year, George Ford may well have timed his dash for Rugby World Cup 2015 absolutely perfectly.

Son of Bath Head Coach Mike Ford, George grew up in Rugby League territory and it was at school in Wigan that he first met his great friend Owen Farrell. The pair's careers have intertwined since then, with a move south and a switch to the XV-a-side game coming naturally to Ford.

Initially in the Leicester Academy, he has thrived since moving to Bath and 2014 was his breakthrough year on the international stage.

Stuart Lancaster decided to blood the playmaker from the bench but he was selected to start the final two matches of 2014. "You're the boss, now get bossing," Lancaster told him and he did just that.

Yet Ford really came of age in 2015, starting every match and ensuring England played an exciting, attacking brand of Rugby that saw them score 18 tries in five matches, with an astonishing 55 points coming against France in their final round of the Tournament.

Not afraid to stand on the gainline and dictate play, Geroge Ford is very much the real deal and he intends to prove that this September.

England appearances: 11
England points: 109

Brad Barritt

England Rugby

A brave and physical centre with defensive skills second to none, Brad Barritt is a reliable and trusted member of Stuart Lancaster's England side.

November 2014 at Twickenham Stadium demonstrates why Stuart Lancaster rates the centre so highly.

There were two minutes left in the Test against Australia. England was winning 26-17, but Quade Cooper for Australia was on the attack.

In stepped Barritt. Though carrying an injury, he commited to a tackle that caused even seasoned Rugby watchers to wince.

No wonder that his Director of Rugby at Saracens, Mark McCall, called his display "one of the bravest and most physical performances I've seen by anyone, never mind a centre".

Such commitment has been Barritt's hallmark since his debut against Scotland in 2012.

Born in Durban, South Africa, Barritt joined Saracens in 2008 and made his England Saxons debut the following year against the USA, scoring a try. In 2010 he played against New Zealand Maori in a non-cap match and was a full international two years later.

In 2012 he scored his first international try in that stunning win over New Zealand which heralded a new dawn under Stuart Lancaster.

Injuries since then have restricted his appearances, but he scored a second international try against South Africa in 2014. He is a reliable and versatile member of Lancaster's squad.

England appearances: 22
England points: 10

Mike Brown

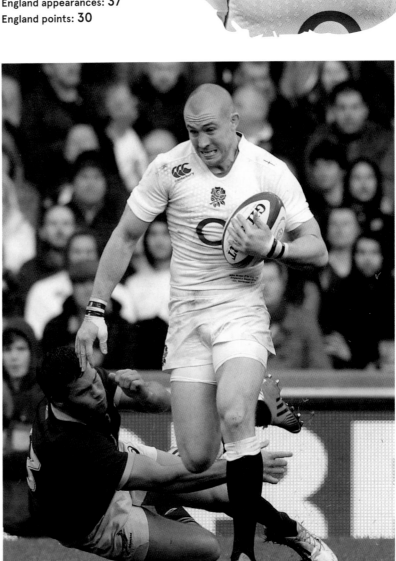

England Rugby

A dynamic, attacking full-back who excels under the high ball, Mike Brown enjoyed a stellar 2013/14 season to make the no. 15 shirt his own.

There comes a time when a player is impossible to ignore and simply demands to be squeezed into the starting XV. For Mike Brown, that time came towards the end of 2012.

Alex Goode was excelling at full-back, but Stuart Lancaster was so keen to bring Brown into the fold he started on the wing against South Africa and New Zealand, his first international Rugby start since 2008.

The switch was a success, but Brown truly began to excel for England the following season, when he switched to his natural position of full-back. In five matches he scored four tries, made 543m and 10 clean breaks, and beat 25 men in what was a stunning tournament on a personal and team level.

Indeed, he started 17 consecutive matches in the position from the tour of South America in the summer of 2013 to the end of the following year, demonstrating his consistency and fitness.

Brown is particularly adept under the high ball, and his elusiveness upon taking a catch is a key weapon, as are his tackling and speed.

With Ben Foden and Alex Goode certain to provide further competition, full-back is an area in which England are extremely strong – but Brown is the man in possession of the shirt.

England appearances: 37
England points: 30

Jonny May

Speed, skill, a step and superb finishing ability mark Jonny May out as one of the most exciting talents in the English Game.

England Rugby

When Jonny May received the ball inside his own half after just three minutes of the Test against New Zealand in November 2014, there didn't seem to be much on. Ahead of him stood Conrad Smith, one of the world's great centres, and behind him full-back Israel Dagg. Eight seconds later May had grounded the ball behind the New Zealand line and was celebrating like a man possessed as Twickenham Stadium rose to acclaim one of the great tries.

It was the perfect example of what the Shed at Gloucester have become used to in recent years – May's directness and speed tearing a top-class defence apart. The wing offers something different, and his creativity and spark are why he has become a vital member of Stuart Lancaster's side.

Born in Swindon in 1990, May came through the England Under-20 side along with a number of Gloucester team-mates such as Freddie Burns, Charlie Sharples and Henry Trinder. Winner of the English Premiership Try of the Year in 2012 he made his England debut in the Tour of Argentina in the summer of 2013 before establishing himself in Lancaster's side during 2014.

Twickenham hopes that extraordinary try against New Zealand was just the start.

England appearances: 13
England points: 15

Anthony Watson

England Rugby

A superb young talent who made his breakthrough into the England side towards the end of 2014, Watson has the world at his feet.

It is fair to say Anthony Watson did not have the easiest introduction to Test Rugby in 2014. On his first two Tests he came up against two of the toughest opponents in world Rugby in the form of Julian Savea and Bryan Habana.

The former had just been described as "probably better" than Jonah Lomu by New Zealand boss Steve Hansen, while Habana has more than a century of caps and almost 300 points in the bank for South Africa. Watson, in contrast, had turned professional only in 2011 and was just 20 years old. It is a sign of his character that he thrived under the pressure, going on to keep his place against Samoa and Australia.

Yet he is not the first Watson to represent England, with older brother Marcus an England Sevens squad member. As if that wasn't enough, a third sibling, Callum, is a young scrum-half tipped for great things at London Irish.

But 2015 is likely to be Anthony's year. He used the early year fixtures to cement his place in the side, scoring his first two international tries against Wales and France as the Junior World Championship 2013 winner demonstrated the footwork and pace that have become familiar to fans of London Irish and Bath. Habana and Savea held no fear for Watson – and neither will the upcoming Tournament.

England appearances: 9
England points: 10

England 21–44 South Africa

DE BEER BRILLIANCE DECISIVE

As in 1995, England exited Rugby World Cup 1999 after a unique demonstration of Rugby brilliance. South African fly-half Jannie de Beer kicked five drop goals in 31 second-half minutes – contributing to his personal total of 34 points – as England came up short in their Rugby World Cup 1999 quarter-final at the Stade de France.

Rugby World Cup 2015 Players to Watch

We know all about the best England has to offer, but what about the rest of the world? Well, they're good – very good, and they are heading to these shores determined to return home with the Webb Ellis Cup.

South Africa's Bryan Habana is tackled by England's Josh Lewsey during a pool match at Rugby World Cup 2007

Introduction

From Richie McCaw to Israel Folau, England will have to beat the best in the world to win Rugby World Cup 2015. Here we profile some of the key men.

Every side has a talisman, a key player the opposition know they have to stop. Sometimes – in the case of Richie McCaw or Thierry Dusautoir – he is the captain, as well as one of the key individuals.

On other occasions, as with George North, Bryan Habana or Israel Folau, he is the deadliest finisher in a side, a player who can change the course of a match or Tournament with one slaloming run.

Then there are the powerhouses, the likes of Paul O'Connell or Richie Gray who work in the engine room, doing the dirty work so the flyers have ammunition to load and fire.

These are the superstars, the box-office hits who will enthral the casual punter and leave rugby aficionados drooling. Right now, every one of them will be dreaming of lifting the Webb Ellis Cup. One of them, New Zealand captain McCaw, has already done so under the greatest pressure imaginable on New Zealand soil in 2011. Keep these men quiet, and the battle will be largely won.

They are all hugely experienced and will be surrounded by a superb supporting cast from Dan Carter to Will Genia, Bismarck du Plessis to Sam Warburton.

But the point of any Rugby World Cup is that it shouldn't be easy to win, and that is due to the presence of men like these on every team. They are the reason no side has ever retained the Webb Ellis Cup, and why few would be fully confident of putting money on any side before the 2015 Tournament has started.

McCaw triumphed despite personal adversity four years ago, but who is to say he can reach the same heights this time around? Will a new world star emerge in George North, and what about his battle with Israel Folau in the pool stages? They have already crossed swords in the Lions series of 2013 and it was an epic confrontation then. The old stagers in Habana and Juan Martín Hernández have been here before of course and know how to win tight Test matches at Rugby World Cups.

These are the players who bring in the crowd and make this Tournament so compelling. They are also the men England must nullify. We can't wait to see them do battle.

Opposite: Scotland lock Richie Gray will be taking part in his second Rugby World Cup and his experience will be invaluable

Below: Wales winger George North has the potential to be one of the stars of the Tournament. England will need to keep a close eye on him in their pool match

Richie McCaw

Arguably the finest player and captain the sport has ever seen, Richie McCaw will be desperate to become the first man to skipper a side to back-to-back Rugby World Cup victories.

When New Zealand beat Wales in their final match of 2014, it took Richie McCaw past a very special milestone. No other player in history has captained a Test side 100 times, and it is very unlikely anyone ever will again. What's more, New Zealand have won 88 of those matches, a quite incredible record.

The undoubted highlight was the victory in Rugby World Cup 2011 on home soil, a Tournament that demonstrated McCaw's incredible leadership and sacrifice for the side.

During pre-season training the flanker fractured a metatarsal in his foot, and had a pin inserted to ensure he made the Tournament. During the pool match against France, in which McCaw became the first New Zealand player to reach a century of caps, he re-aggravated the injury. Unable to train or play in the final pool match against Canada, McCaw decided against having an x-ray and instead played in all the knockout matches, including the Final. A scan after the Tournament showed he had played three matches with a broken foot.

McCaw has not taken a backwards step since making his debut against Ireland in 2001 despite having played just 17 matches for Canterbury. He was named Man of the Match and was given a standing ovation.

In 2006, he was appointed New Zealand captain. There is no finer competitor in world Rugby.

The highly experienced Richie McCaw led New Zealand to Rugby World Cup victory in 2011 and in November 2014 became the first Union player to achieve 100 caps as captain

Israel Folau

A former Australian Rules Football and Rugby League superstar who is now taking Union by storm, Israel Folau is one of Australia's key men.

Israel Folau! What a talent, what a star, what a player!

Israel Folau has already conquered Rugby League, he has already excelled in Australian Rules Football and now he is one of the finest players in Rugby Union. In fact, most sportsmen would be happy to have matched Folau's achievements in one sport, but he is already breaking records in his third.

Just 17 when he made his Rugby League debut for Melbourne Storm back in 2007, he broke the record for most tries by a rookie in his debut season before becoming the youngest player to represent Australia in the sport.

Not satisfied with that, he switched to AFL with Greater Western Sydney, before deciding to try a third code in the summer of 2012 with his move to Union and the New South Wales Waratahs.

Selected to make his Australia debut in the first Test against the Lions in the summer of 2013, he made an immediate impact, scoring two stunning tries in a losing cause.

Folau went on to equal Lote Tuqiri's tally of 10 tries in a season in 2013, while his record of 11 tries in 13 Tests between October 2013 and September of the following year shows both his threat and consistency.

Now a full-back and one of the first names on the Australia team sheet, Folau is pure box office.

Israel Folau has excelled in Rugby League, Australian Rules Football and Rugby Union. The full-back has an eye for a try and is sure to light up Rugby World Cup 2015

Bryan Habana

Over a century of caps in an international career that has now spanned more than a decade, Bryan Habana is one of the finest wings in Rugby history.

Bryan Habana could have retired from Rugby in 2007 and still gone down as one of the finest players in the history of the Game. Named IRB Player of the Year after his performances for South Africa's Rugby World Cup-winning side, the wing scored eight tries to match Jonah Lomu's record set in 1995.

But Habana has always enjoyed a good sense of timing. He scored with his first touch in Test Rugby against England at Twickenham Stadium in 2004, as the former age-group centre and scrum-half demonstrated that moving to the wing really would be the making of him.

In 2005 he scored 12 tries in as many Tests, including two stunning long-distance efforts against Australia as South Africa won their first Tri-Nations match away from home in seven years.

But it was in 2007 that he shook the world, both for the Bulls and then by scoring four tries in two Tests against England. If that wasn't enough he raced a cheetah at a promotional event (one of the very rare occasions he would taste defeat) before he dominated Rugby World Cup 2007, scoring four tries against Samoa, two against USA and a further double in the semi-final against Argentina.

He went on to score a memorable try against the Lions in 2009 and then broke South Africa's try-scoring record during Rugby World Cup 2011.

Sprinkbok winger Bryan Habana is a prolific try scorer and scored eight tries at Rugby World Cup 2007. He scored two more tries in 2011

Juan Martín Hernández

"The Magician" has been a mainstay in the Argentina side since 2003 and is perhaps the most exciting player South America has produced.

Juan Martín Hernández made his debut in the 144–0 defeat of Paraguay in 2003, but really came to prominence upon moving to Europe with Stade Français the same year. In Paris he developed a reputation as a classy, skilful full-back with superb defensive skills.

As such it was a surprise to see him line up at fly-half for Argentina's opener against France in their opening match of Rugby World Cup 2007, but as with almost everything coach Marcello Loffreda did in that Tournament, it was to be an inspired decision. Argentina beat the hosts on their own turf and Hernández continued in the position throughout the Tournament, landing three drop goals in the decisive pool match against Ireland and another in the quarter-final win over Scotland.

The Argentines brave run ended in defeat to eventual winners South Africa at the semi-final stage, but Hernández had done enough to be included on the shortlist for IRB Player of the Year.

A knee injury suffered in March 2011 forced Hernández to miss the remainder of that season and the subsequent Rugby World Cup. But over the course of 2013 and 2014 he kick-started his international career again, playing seven matches in the centre and one at fly-half to prove the magician still has another trick or two up his sleeve.

Argentina centre Juan Martín Hernández missed out on Rugby World Cup 2011 through injury but is back in the Argentina side for the 2015 Tournament

Thierry Dusautoir

France's inspirational captain is a former IRB Player of the Year who consistently produces his best at Rugby World Cups.

It was perhaps the finest performance from a forward in Rugby World Cup history.

France against New Zealand in the 2007 quarter-final was expected to be relatively straightforward for Northern Hemisphere side, and when they raced into a 13–0 lead that seemed likely to be the case. But Dusautoir, who was only in the squad due to an injury to Elvis Vermeulen – put in a superb perfomance and left New Zealand all shook up.

The flanker not only scored the try that brought France back into the match, he made 38 tackles, setting a new world record in the process. By contrast, the entire New Zealand side made just 36 tackles during the match.

He certainly enjoys playing New Zealand. Four years later he led a French side that had seemingly been in disarray to the Final, where he was named Man of the Match for scoring a try and making 21 tackles in his side's 8–7 defeat.

He was named IRB Player of the Year in 2011, a year after leading France to their first Grand Slam since 2004, and it says it all that Richie McCaw rates the Frenchman as his toughest opponent.

A captain who leads by example, he has become one of the most impressive leaders and characters in the Game. With an unpredictable French side tipped by many to come good in 2015, Dusautoir will be central to their ambitions.

A former IRB Player of the Year, Thierry Dusautoir is respected throughout the Game and his leadership will be crucial if France are to progress

George North

One of the most exciting and talented players in world Rugby, North could well be the star of Rugby World Cup 2015.

We knew within five minutes that George North was destined to be a star. Aged just 18 years and 214 days, the giant wing was picked to make his international debut against South Africa at the Millennium Stadium, and he was simply unplayable.

He scored after five minutes and again after half-time, becoming the youngest ever player to score two tries on their international debut against a major Union.

Wales may have lost the Test, but that was just the start for North as he has developed into a world-class player.

Australia certainly will not be looking forward to facing him in their Rugby World Cup 2015 pool match, with memories of his displays against them for the Lions in 2013 still fresh in the mind. His try in the opening Test was one of the best ever scored by a Lion, while in the second he decided to pick up would-be tackler Israel Folau – all 102kg of him – and carry him on his back before dumping him to the ground in one of the moments of the tour. If that wasn't enough, he then scored another try in the third Test to announce himself as a global superstar.

One of the finest backs in world Rugby, North could find that 2015 is his year.

Wales back George North is a prodigious talent. Many will be looking for him to transfer his form of recent years to the stage of Rugby World Cup 2015

Paul O'Connell

One of the most inspirational forwards in Irish Rugby history, Paul O'Connell is a former Lions captain who is still at the peak of his powers.

Paul O'Connell and Brian O'Driscoll have been the two talismanic figures at the forefront of Irish Rugby for the last 15 years. O'Driscoll may have retired, but O'Connell is still there, working away at the coalface. He will turn 36 during Rugby World Cup 2015, but many claim he is producing the finest Game of his career.

Surely, O'Connell can no longer have any regrets about turning down a potential swimming career in favour of Rugby.

A Munster legend, he made his international debut in 2002 and was an integral member of the 2005 Lions side. Triple crowns followed for Ireland in 2006 and 2007, with his Man of the Match display against England in the latter year one of his very finest performances.

But it was in 2009 that O'Connell and Ireland took a giant leap forward, winning their first Grand Slam in 61 years after an emotional victory at the Millennium Stadium in their final match. O'Connell was rewarded with the Lions captaincy for the tour of South Africa, and he started in all three Tests.

Though injury ruled him out of the last two Tests, he was still first choice for the 2013 Lions. O'Connell's character is summed up by the fact he stayed with the team to help guide them through the last few weeks of the tour and to a famous series victory. Now he hopes for one last hurrah.

Ireland captain Paul O'Connell is playing some of the best Rugby of his career and he will be looking to extend his rich form into Rugby World Cup 2015

Richie Gray

The most high-profile of Scotland's new generation, Richie Gray is a hugely talented lock who made a big impact on the 2013 Lions tour.

You can't really miss Richie Gray. Standing at well over 2m tall and with a shock of blond hair, he catches the eye wherever he is on the field – and that generally happens to be at the centre of the action.

Alongside brother Jonny, full-back Stuart Hogg, fly-half Finn Russell and wing Tim Visser, Gray is playing a vital role in re-establishing Scotland as a force to be reckoned with under new coach Vern Cotter.

A regular in Scotland's age-group sides, Gray was first called up by Andy Robinson for the 2010 November internationals, establishing himself as a huge talent with two Man of the Match displays in the Six Nations a few months later.

He started every match in Rugby World Cup 2011 and seemed a certainty for the Lions in 2013 until a hamstring injury against Wales ended his Six Nations and put his place in Warren Gatland's tour party at risk. But Gatland's faith in Gray was such that he took him to Australia despite a lack of playing time in the months leading up to the tour, and the second row made his Lions debut in the final, victorious, Test.

By the following November brother Jonny was on the scene replacing Richie to make his international debut against South Africa. They became the 22nd set of brothers to play for Scotland together against Argentina a year later.

Richie Gray has strength and pace and is one of Scotland's rising stars. He played every one of Scotland's Rugby World Cup 2011 matches and has starred for the Lions

England 20-17 Australia

WILKINSON KICKS ENGLAND TO GLORY IN RUGBY WORLD CUP 2003

Only seconds of extra-time were left when Jonny Wilkinson supplied one of Rugby's iconic images, his weaker right foot striking the decisive drop goal that finally exhausted Australia's defiance. England should have put the match to bed within 80 minutes but were unable to finish off a resilient Australia side – but then Wilkinson settled the matter with a kick heard round the world as England triumphed at the Telstra Stadium in Sydney.

Stuart Lancaster and the England Coaching Team

England Rugby

The team who make the decisions and pick the side, Stuart Lancaster, Andy Farrell, Graham Rowntree and Mike Catt, will be as vital as any player at the Tournament.

After Rugby World Cup 2011, English Rugby looked for a fresh start and a new figurehead. Following Martin Johnson's departure, the RFU looked within and asked Stuart Lancaster, the Saxons' coach and Head of Elite Player Development, to take charge on a temporary basis. It proved to be an inspired choice. It is now impossible to imagine English Rugby without the Cumbrian former school teacher in charge, and he has brought about a change in philosophy and attitude within the sport.

Key to Lancaster's approach is culture, and his young side embodies his values: hard work, teamwork and organisation. A straight talker whose openness and honesty has been appreciated by the players, press and public at large, Lancaster has revelled in his position.

He has chosen his lieutenants wisely, too, with three former England players of some repute assisting him in the meticulous preparations put in place from the team's Pennyhill Park base.

Graham Rowntree has been a member of the England coaching set-up since 2008, having won 54 England caps and played in two Rugby World Cups during an 11-year international career at prop. Given responsibility for the forwards, he was hailed by South African counterpart Johann van Graan as "one of the best in the world" in November 2014, and it is not hard

to see why. Under his guidance the England pack has become one of the finest around, while he was also part of the coaching team on the Lions tours of 2009 and 2013.

Andy Farrell was approached by Lancaster to become part of his coaching team in December 2011, and his appointment has been a stunning success. A legend in Rugby League, Farrell – father of England fly-half Owen – converted to Union in 2005 and was a member of the England squad that reached the Final of Rugby World Cup 2007. Moving into coaching with Saracens upon retirement he was made a permanent

"If we try out an idea in training and the players don't like it then it'll be dropped. The players drive it all. That's the relationship Stuart and we have with them at the moment. There's a massive amount of trust."

England Attacking Skills Coach, Mike Catt

member of the England set-up in the summer of 2012. His stock has risen to such an extent he was asked by Warren Gatland to join Rowntree as a member of his coaching staff for the 2013 Lions tour to Australia, which Farrell did with distinction.

The final member of Lancaster's staff is Mike Catt. The Attacking Skills Coach scored 142 points in an England shirt, featuring in 75 England and one Lions test between 1994 and 2007. The man who kicked the ball to touch in the final act of the Final of Rugby

World Cup 2003 became the oldest man to feature in a Final four years later, aged 36 years and one month. After moving into coaching with London Irish, he was asked to assist on the tour to South Africa in the summer of 2012 before being appointed a permanent member of staff.

Under Lancaster all three have formed a unit that has evolved alongside the team they have constructed. Now they face their toughest test, but it's one they are well prepared for.

Opposite: Andy Farrell, Graham Rowntree, Stuart Lancaster and Mike Catt are the key members of the England management team

Above: England Head Coach Stuart Lancaster is renowned for his straight talking and honesty

England 14-9 France

ENGLAND REACH SECOND SUCCESSIVE FINAL

Josh Lewsey's dramatic score after just 78 seconds of the semi-final against hosts France in Paris set the tone as England upset the odds to reach their second successive Rugby World Cup Final. Lewsey pounced as Damien Traille dithered, and Jonny Wilkinson landed a penalty and a drop goal in the last five minutes as England stunned the French.

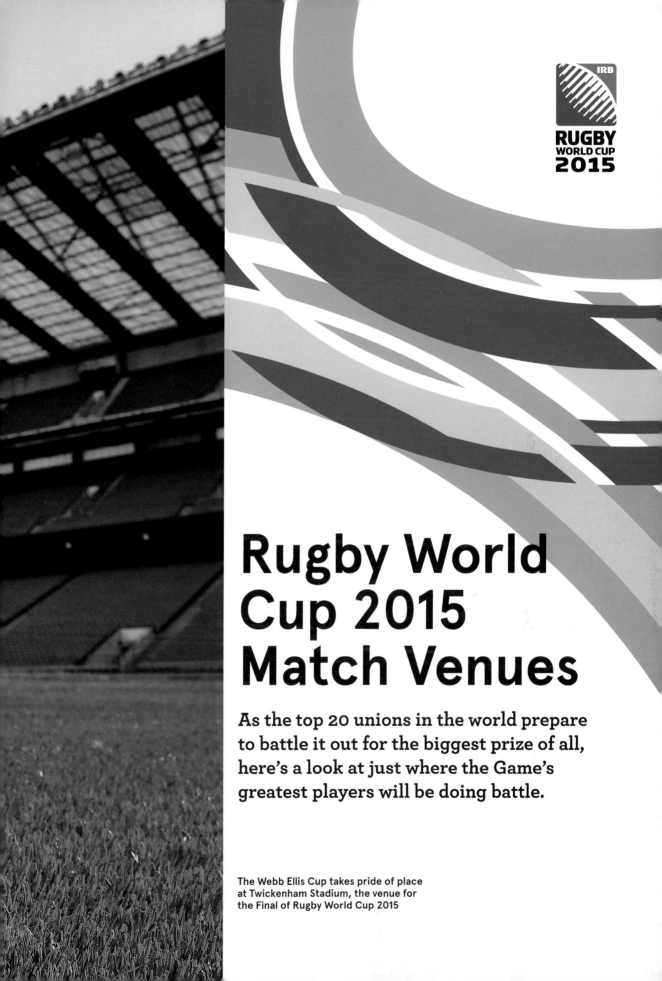

Rugby World Cup 2015 Match Venues

As the top 20 unions in the world prepare to battle it out for the biggest prize of all, here's a look at just where the Game's greatest players will be doing battle.

The Webb Ellis Cup takes pride of place at Twickenham Stadium, the venue for the Final of Rugby World Cup 2015

RUGBY WORLD CUP 2015

Rugby World Cup 2015 Venues

In total, 13 venues from England and Cardiff will play host as 20 unions descend for the biggest competition in world Rugby.

Just one glance at the venues for Rugby World Cup 2015 should leave supporters in no doubt about the scale of the Tournament. Since the first Rugby World Cup in 1987, the Game of Rugby has changed no end and the grounds themselves perhaps show this more than anything. Rugby World Cup 2015 will see state-of-the-art stadiums open their doors to fans from across the world.

The eye is naturally drawn to the likes of Wembley Stadium. The home of English football boasts a capacity of 90,000 and has hosted some of the biggest sporting events in the world, including the 1966 FIFA World Cup Final. The Millennium Stadium is another venue sure to have spectators salivating. With the roof closed and the lights on, there are few grounds that can compete with the special atmosphere generated in the 74,154-seater stadium in Cardiff. The Stadium, Queen Elizabeth Olympic Park completes an impressive trio of awe-inspiring venues, with the home of London's Olympic Games opening its doors to the world of sport once more.

The beauty of the stadiums in use at Rugby World Cup 2015 lies in the variety on offer. While venues such as Wembley Stadium and the Millennium Stadium will play host, so will the likes of Kingsholm and Sandy Park. The pair are the homes of Gloucester and Exeter and their presence among the 13 venues pays tribute to the growing strength of English club rugby.

Football grounds too will get ready to welcome Rugby's biggest superstars. St James' Park, Manchester City Stadium and Villa Park are just three of the eight football grounds which will offer supporters an alternative experience.

At the centre of the 13 stadiums on show at Rugby World Cup 2015 is Twickenham Stadium, the home of English Rugby. There are few venues that can compete with the history of the 82,000-seater stadium, the biggest dedicated Rugby ground in the world. Host to the Final of Rugby World Cup 1991, Twickenham Stadium is once again gearing up for the biggest match in Rugby. The last Final at Twickenham Stadium saw Australia lift the Trophy. Could this be England's time for glory?

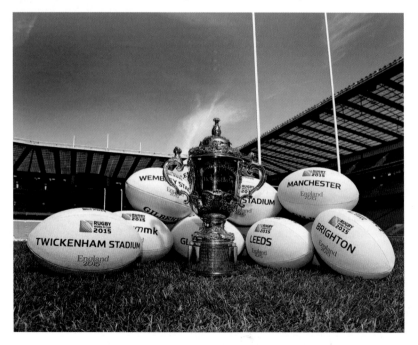

Thirteen high-class stadiums will be used during the six weeks of Rugby World Cup 2015

NEWCASTLE

LEEDS

MANCHESTER

LEICESTER

BIRMINGHAM

MILTON KEYNES

GLOUCESTER

WEMBLEY

CARDIFF

TWICKENHAM

STRATFORD

BRIGHTON

EXETER

Twickenham Stadium

The largest dedicated Rugby stadium in the world will host 10 matches during Rugby World Cup 2015, including the Final.

The home of English Rugby, Twickenham Stadium has become a vital part of Rugby history. Opened in 1909 it hosted its first ever match that year, with Harlequins taking on Richmond in a local derby. Just one year later Twickenham went on to host its first ever international match, as England defeated Wales for the first time in 12 years.

Over a century on from that match it has gone on to host countless matches, as well as music concerts for the likes of the Rolling Stones.

Twickenham Stadium has hosted the Final of Rugby World Cup before, back in 1991, and it will once again for the 2015 Tournament.

Nine other matches will also be taking place at the 82,000-seater stadium, including both of the semi-finals. Hosts England will play three of their four pool matches at Twickenham, including their crunch clashes against Australia and Wales.

Since the turn of the century the stadium has undergone major renovations. The South Stand has had its capacity increased, meaning the venue now holds 82,000 as opposed to its previous 75,000.

The biggest dedicated Rugby ground in the world, there are few stadiums in the world that can rival Twickenham. Not only does the home of English Rugby boast unrivalled facilities for fans, the venue has not forgotten its prestigious history. The World Rugby Union museum is located in the ground and offers supporters the opportunity to trace the history of the sport.

Opposite: The Final of Rugby World Cup 2015 as well as nine other matches will be hosted at Twickenham Stadium

Below: Twickenham Stadium has an 82,000 seat-capacity and is the largest stadium in the world dedicated to Rugby

"The world's best players will now have a chance to play in some of the world's best stadiums and supporters can look forward to a feast of Rugby. It's almost enough to bring me out of retirement!"

Lawrence Dallaglio, former England captain and Rugby World Cup 2003 winner

Brighton Community Stadium

Built in 2011 and with a capacity of over 30,000, the Brighton Community Stadium will host two matches from Pool B.

The home of Brighton & Hove Albion Football Club, the stadium is one of the newest in the United Kingdom. Built at a cost of £93 million, the venue provided a permanent home for the club after 12 years in temporary accommodation at the Withdean Stadium.

With its own train station and only an hour's journey from London, the stadium in Sussex has earned praise for its modern design which provides fans with brilliant views of the pitch and padded seating.

During the Tournament the Brighton Community Stadium will host two

Rugby World Cup 2015 matches.

Local fans will be excited by the arrival of two-time Rugby World Cup Champions South Africa, who will take on Japan at the Brighton Community Stadium, while surprise package Samoa will also face the ever-improving USA there.

More than 30,000 supporters will fill the Brighton Community Stadium to see two Rugby World Cup 2015 matches – South Africa v Japan and Samoa v USA

Elland Road

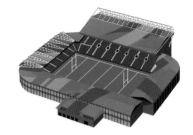

One of England's most famous football grounds will prepare to welcome Rugby for the first time since 1992.

Elland Road, Leeds, may be situated in the heartland of Rugby League, but it will now host two Rugby Union matches during the Tournament. Italy will take on Canada in their Pool D match, while Scotland will face the USA in their Pool B clash.

Union has only featured once at the stadium before, back in 1992 when South Africa played a North of England Rugby team. On that occasion 14,000 fans turned out to watch the spectacle, but the venue has a capacity of nearly 38,000.

Given its history and traditional design, Elland Road will provide Rugby fans with an alternative experience to other venues at Rugby World Cup 2015.

The ground has previously hosted Rugby League matches, with the Tri-Nations final and the Rugby League Four Nations final both taking place there with crowds of over 25,000 since the turn of the century.

The famous ground of Leeds United Football Club, Elland Road has a capacity of more than 37,000 and a rich history that dates back to 1919. The venue will host Italy v Canada and Scotland v USA

Kingsholm

Home of Gloucester Rugby Club, Kingsholm was a venue when England co-hosted Rugby World Cup 1991.

Regarded as one of the noisiest grounds in English Rugby, Kingsholm is sure to provide fans with a memorable Rugby World Cup 2015. With a capacity of 16,500, the Gloucester ground is one of the smallest in the competition, but its atmosphere more than makes up for its size.

The stadium was used as one of the venues for Rugby World Cup 1991, hosting New Zealand's 43–6 win over the USA. That was its sole match during the Tournament, but this time around four will take place there.

Tonga will take on Georgia, while Scotland will come up against Japan at Kingsholm, too. Excitingly for fans, Argentina will also take to the field against Georgia. The South American union made the quarter-finals at Rugby World Cup 2011 and finished third in 2007. Kingsholm's matches are rounded off with a clash between USA and Japan.

Kingsholm is likely to be one of the most atmospheric Rugby World Cup 2015 venues. The stadium will play host to such fascinating Tournament matches as Tonga v Georgia, Scotland v Japan, Argentina v Georgia and USA v Japan

Leicester City Stadium

Opened in 2002, the Leicester City Stadium boasts a capacity of over 32,000 and will host three Rugby World Cup 2015 matches.

Located just a stone's throw away from Welford Road, the home of Leicester Tigers Rugby Club, the Leicester City Stadium is sure to be a hotbed of supporters during Rugby World Cup 2015.

The state-of-the-art venue has hosted Rugby matches before and Leicester Tigers have played Heineken Cup quarter-finals and semi-finals there, while South Africa also competed against a World XV in 2006 at the stadium. The ground is the 19th largest in England and will host three matches during the Tournament. Argentina are scheduled to play there twice, against Tonga and Namibia, while Canada and Romania are also due to meet at the Leicester stadium.

As well as hosting international Rugby, the venue has previously hosted international football – including five-times World Champions Brazil.

The Leicester City Stadium will host three Rugby World Cup 2015 matches: Argentina v Tonga, Argentina v Namibia and Canada v Romania

Manchester City Stadium

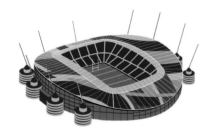

The home of 2013/14 Premier League champions Manchester City, the stadium is another modern ground which highlights the quality of venues on offer at Rugby World Cup 2015.

Constructed for the 2002 Commonwealth Games, the stadium is located just 10 minutes from Manchester city centre. It currently has a capacity of 47,800, but Manchester City's ambitious Abu Dhabi owners have made plans to expand it to 55,000.

The venue has hosted Rugby before when New Zealand played Fiji in the Final of the Rugby Sevens at the Commonwealth Games. It also became the first English city to host the Rugby League Magic Weekend from 2012 to 2014. The festival of Rugby saw seven matches take place

at the stadium over the course of two days.

At Rugby World Cup 2015, the Manchester City Stadium will host just one match, England's final pool match against Uruguay. Home fans will be hoping that the stadium sees England progress to the knock out stages.

The home of Manchester City Football Club, this state-of-the art Rugby World Cup 2015 venue will host England's final pool match against Uruguay

Millennium Stadium

The home of Welsh Rugby will play host to eight matches during Rugby World Cup 2015, including two quarter-finals and France's clash with Ireland.

There are few sporting arenas that can rival the Millennium Stadium when it comes to size and atmosphere. With the roof shut, belted verses of 'Delilah' are enough to deafen anyone. Add to that the steep seating and brilliant views, and you have one of the best sporting venues in the world.

With a capacity of 74,154 the Millennium is set to welcome over half a million Rugby fans during the Tournament. In total eight matches will be taking place at the venue, including two quarter-finals.

Wales are scheduled to play at the Millennium Stadium twice during the Tournament against Uruguay and Fiji in their Pool A matches.

The pick of the pool matches will see European heavyweights France and Ireland play. Ireland reached the quarter-finals at Rugby World Cup 2011, while France went down 8–7 to the hosts New Zealand in the Final.

The Millennium Stadium in Cardiff holds 74,154 and is regarded as one of the world's greatest Rugby venues. The stadium will host two of Wales's pool matches and Ireland v France

The Stadium,
Queen Elizabeth Olympic Park

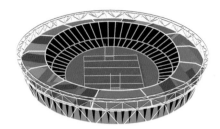

The centre of the London Olympic Games in 2012 will now open its doors once again, this time to Rugby World Cup 2015.

Built for the 2012 Olympic Games, the 54,000-seater stadium is set to become the new home of West Ham United Football Club in 2016.

The venue is the newest of all those on offer at Rugby World Cup 2015 and boasts several state-of-the-art features.

During the 2012 Olympic Games the stadium played host to some spectacular sporting events, including Super Saturday – where Mo Farah, Jessica Ennis-Hill and Greg Rutherford all won gold.

Organisers will expect more magical moments during the Tournament and with France, Ireland, New Zealand and South Africa all playing there, they won't be disappointed.

As well as welcoming four of the world's biggest teams during the pool stages, the The Stadium, Queen Elizabeth Olympic Park is also set to host the Bronze Final.

The Stadium, Queen Elizabeth Olympic Park is likely to be one of the most popular during the Tournament. The Rugby World Cup 2015 venue will host matches featuring France, Ireland, New Zealand and South Africa

Sandy Park

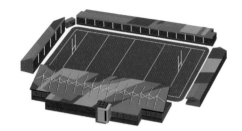

Just as the Exeter Chiefs have grown as a force, so has their home, the ever-expanding Sandy Park.

Constructed in 2006 for just £15 million, Sandy Park has undergone huge developments since then. It was originally built to hold 8,000, then in 2012 came the announcement that a five-year plan was in place to expand the stadium to a 20,600 capacity.

The first phase of the redevelopment was carried out in the summer of 2014 at a cost of £10 million and means the ground now holds 12,300 – its capacity for Rugby World Cup 2015.

Just as Sandy Park has been going from strength to strength, so have the Exeter Chiefs. After gaining promotion to the Premiership in 2010, the Chiefs have established themselves as a regular in the division.

During Rugby World Cup 2015, the ground will play host to three matches, including Six Nations side Italy's clash with Romania.

Sandy Park is the home of the English Rugby side Exeter Chiefs. The 12,300-capacity venue will host three matches at Rugby World Cup 2015, including Italy v Romania

St James' Park

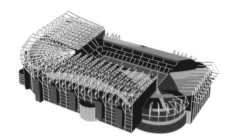

The home of Newcastle United Football Club, St James' Park will be one of the most atmospheric grounds at the Tournament.

Based in Newcastle's city centre, there are few stadiums that can compete with the atmosphere and buzz of St James' Park on a matchday. In 2015 it will be playing host to plenty of Rugby from both codes, for as well as having three Rugby World Cup 2015 matches, the stadium is set to welcome the stars of Rugby League for the Magic Weekend.

For Rugby World Cup 2015, fans visiting the ground will be in for a treat, as Rugby World Cup 2007 champions South Africa take on Scotland. With it just being a short drive across the border, the Scots are sure to have vocal support in front of a packed crowd.

Reigning champions New Zealand also have one pool match in Newcastle as they take on Tonga. Like Scotland's two matches there, New Zealand's visit is sure to delight fans at the 52,409-seater stadium in one of England's most vibrant cities.

St James' Park will host three Rugby World Cup 2015 matches. The pick of these matches is arguably South Africa v Scotland and New Zealand's pool match against Tonga

Stadium MK

**RUGBY
WORLD CUP
2015**

**Previously host to Heineken Cup matches,
Milton Keynes is now getting ready to welcome
fans for Rugby World Cup 2015.**

Stadium MK is no stranger to Rugby. Although home to the MK Dons, the ground has hosted Heineken Cup matches for Northampton Saints and Premiership matches for Saracens.

In 2011, the Saints took on Ulster in front of 21,309 supporters, but for this Tournament there will be 30,717 fans packed in to watch the likes of 2011 runners-up France. The Six Nations side's visit to Milton Keynes is the pick of the three ties taking place in the town, as they take on Canada in their Pool D match.

But supporters will also enjoy the visits of Fiji and Samoa, who play Uruguay and Japan respectively. Both the south sea islanders will be desperate for victory to prolong their Tournaments.

The stadium itself is one of the newest in the country, having been built in 2007, and expanded as MK Dons have risen through the divisions.

Thirty thousand fans will pack out the Stadium MK on matchdays during Rugby World Cup 2015. The venue will witness Samoa v Japan, France v Canada and Fiji v Uruguay

Villa Park

The home of Aston Villa FC for over a century, Villa Park will now prepare to welcome the Game's biggest stars from the world of Rugby.

There are few stadia that can boast quite as prestigious a history as Villa Park. Over the years it has hosted all manner of sports, from athletics to boxing, and is the home of Aston Villa, holding a capacity of 42,785.

For Rugby World Cup 2015 it will welcome two of the Game's great heavyweights – Australia and South Africa. The Southern Hemisphere giants both have pool matches at Villa Park, providing fans in the Midlands with the opportunity to see some of the Game's greatest players.

The stadium is no stranger to hosting big matches, having previously held the UEFA Cup Winners' Cup final in 1999. Villa Park can also boast a history of Rugby, having welcomed teams from both sides of the code before. It's also been a music venue: Bruce Springsteen and Bon Jovi have both played shows here.

Villa Park will play host to Rugby World Cup 2015 pool matches featuring the Southern Hemisphere giants Australia and South Africa

Wembley Stadium

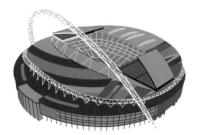

England internationals, the Olympic Games and the Champions League final have all taken place at Wembley – now Rugby World Cup joins the party.

It may be a strange thought for some fans, the idea of Rugby players running out on to the pitch at Wembley Stadium – the home of English football. But in fact, the venue is more than used to hosting the sport. In 2015, a match between Harlequins and Saracens broke the record for the largest ever club Rugby crowd, with 84,068 spectators present.

The stadium itself can hold 90,000 fans and promises to be one of the standout venues of the Tournament.

Big events go hand in hand with Wembley. From sold-out concerts to Champions League finals, the iconic venue has done it all. Hosting Rugby World Cup 2015 matches will tick another box and fans travelling to the stadium are certainly in for a treat.

Although Wembley will host only two matches, one of those is New Zealand v Argentina – one of the toughest pool matches in the Tournament.

One of Rugby World Cup 2015's most hotly anticipated pool matches, New Zealand v Argentina, will be played at the 90,000-capacity Wembley Stadium

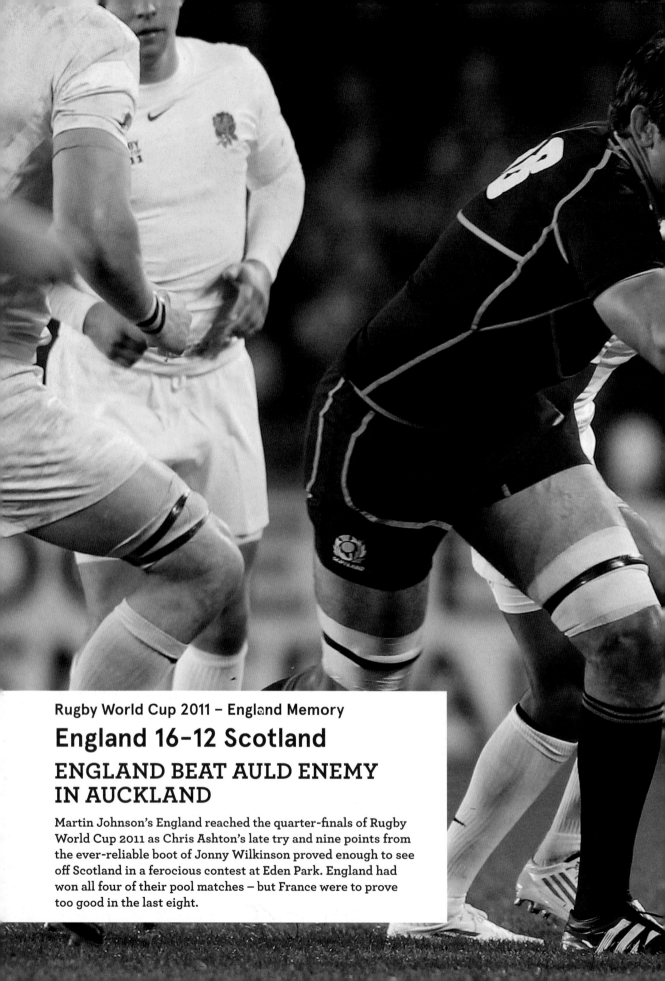

England 16–12 Scotland

ENGLAND BEAT AULD ENEMY IN AUCKLAND

Martin Johnson's England reached the quarter-finals of Rugby World Cup 2011 as Chris Ashton's late try and nine points from the ever-reliable boot of Jonny Wilkinson proved enough to see off Scotland in a ferocious contest at Eden Park. England had won all four of their pool matches – but France were to prove too good in the last eight.

Rugby World Cup 2015 Progress Chart

POOL A

September 18	20:00	Twickenham Stadium, London
England		**Fiji**

September 20	14:30	Millennium Stadium, Cardiff
Wales		**Uruguay**

September 23	16:45	Millennium Stadium, Cardiff
Australia		**Fiji**

September 26	20:00	Twickenham Stadium, London
England		**Wales**

September 27	12:00	Villa Park, Birmingham
Australia		**Uruguay**

October 1	16:45	Millennium Stadium, Cardiff
Wales		**Fiji**

October 3	20:00	Twickenham Stadium, London
England		**Australia**

October 6	20:00	Stadium MK, Milton Keynes
Fiji		**Uruguay**

October 10	16:45	Twickenham Stadium, London
Australia		**Wales**

October 10	20:00	Manchester City Stadium
England		**Uruguay**

FINAL POOL A TABLE

Pos	Team	P	W	L	D	PF	PA	Pts
A1								
A2								
A3								
A4								
A5								

POOL B

September 19	16:45	Brighton Community Stadium
South Africa		**Japan**

September 20	12:00	Brighton Community Stadium
Samoa		**United States**

September 23	14:30	Kingsholm, Gloucester
Scotland		**Japan**

September 26	16:45	Villa Park, Birmingham
South Africa		**Samoa**

September 27	14:30	Elland Road, Leeds
Scotland		**United States**

October 3	14:30	Stadium MK, Milton Keynes
Samoa		**Japan**

October 3	16:45	St James' Park, Newcastle
South Africa		**Scotland**

October 7	16:45	The Stadium, Queen Elizabeth Olympic Park
South Africa		**United States**

October 10	14:30	St James' Park, Newcastle
Samoa		**Scotland**

October 11	20:00	Kingsholm, Gloucester
United States		**Japan**

FINAL POOL B TABLE

Pos	Team	P	W	L	D	PF	PA	Pts
B1								
B2								
B3								
B4								
B5								

All kick-offs listed in local time.

POOL C

September 19	12:00	Kingsholm, Gloucester
Tonga		**Georgia**

September 20	16:45	Wembley Stadium, London
New Zealand		**Argentina**

24 September	20:00	The Stadium, Queen Elizabeth Olympic Park
New Zealand		**Namibia**

September 25	16:45	Kingsholm, Gloucester
Argentina		**Georgia**

September 29	16:45	Sandy Park, Exeter
Tonga		**Namibia**

October 2	20:00	Millennium Stadium, Cardiff
New Zealand		**Georgia**

October 4	14:30	Leicester City Stadium
Argentina		**Tonga**

October 7	20:00	Sandy Park, Exeter
Namibia		**Georgia**

October 9	20:00	St James' Park, Newcastle
New Zealand		**Tonga**

October 11	12:00	Leicester City Stadium
Argentina		**Namibia**

FINAL POOL C TABLE

Pos	Team	P	W	L	D	PF	PA	Pts
C1								
C2								
C3								
C4								
C5								

POOL D

September 19	14:30	Millennium Stadium, Cardiff
Ireland		**Canada**

September 19	20:00	Twickenham, London
France		**Italy**

September 23	20:00	The Stadium, Queen Elizabeth Olympic Park
France		**Romania**

September 26	14:30	Elland Road, Leeds
Italy		**Canada**

September 27	16:45	Wembley Stadium, London
Ireland		**Romania**

October 1	20:00	Stadium MK, Milton Keynes
France		**Canada**

October 4	16:45	The Stadium, Queen Elizabeth Olympic Park
Ireland		**Italy**

October 6	16:45	Leicester City Stadium
Canada		**Romania**

October 11	14:30	Sandy Park, Exeter
Italy		**Romania**

October 11	16:45	Millennium Stadium, Cardiff
France		**Ireland**

FINAL POOL D TABLE

Pos	Team	P	W	L	D	PF	PA	Pts
D1								
D2								
D3								
D4								
D5								

QUARTER-FINALS

QF1	October 17	16:00	Twickenham Stadium, London
	B1		A2

QF2	October 17	20:00	Millennium Stadium, Cardiff
	C1		D2

QF3	October 18	13:00	Millennium Stadium, Cardiff
	D1		C2

QF4	October 18	16:00	Twickenham Stadium, London
	A1		B2

SEMI-FINALS

SF1	October 24	16:00	Twickenham Stadium, London
	Winner QF1		Winner QF2

SF2	October 25	16:00	Twickenham Stadium, London
	Winner QF3		Winner QF4

BRONZE FINAL

October 30	20:00	The Stadium, Queen Elizabeth Olympic Park
Runner-up SF1		Runner-up SF2

RUGBY WORLD CUP 2015 FINAL

October 31	16:00	Twickenham Stadium, London
Winner SF1		Winner SF2

Credits

The publishers would like to thank the following sources for their kind permission to reproduce the pictures in this book.

Getty Images: /Shaun Botterill: 25, 31T, 104-105, 115; /Gabriel Bouys/AFP: 27B; /Simon Bruty: 60-61; /Andrew Cowie/AFP: 111; /Paul Ellis/AFP: 22, 62-63; /Stu Forster: 16-17, 27T, 28, 31B, 94, 99, 121; /Gallo Images: 43; /Paul Gilham: 84B; /Laurence Griffiths: 68B, 70B, 82B, 123; /Stuart Hannagan: 36; /Mike Hewitt: 46, 52; /Clint Hughes: 122; /David Jones: 114; /Glyn Kirk/AFP: 112; /Mark Kolbe: 65; /Alex Livesey: 44, 54, 90; /Philippe Lopez/AFP: 29, 91; /Jamie McDonald: 95; /Chris McGrath: 64; /Marty Melville/AFP: 48; /Sandra Mu: 7, 98; /Dan Mullan: 119; /Kazuhiro Nogi/AFP: 11; /Hannah Peters: 26, 40, 97; /Ryan Pierse: 42, 51; /Popperfoto: 86-87; /Pablo Porciuncula/AFP: 32; /David Rogers: 56-57, 88, 96, 100-101, 106-107, 108, 124-125; /Miguel Rojo/AFP: 33; /Clive Rose: 73B, 118; /Cameron Spencer: 45, 49, 53; /Michael Steele: 117; /Bob Thomas: 34-35, 38-39; /Paul Thomas: 113, 116; /Dave Thompson: 120; /Phil Walter: 50, 55, 92, 128; /Ian Walton: 110; /Anton Want: 37; /William West/AFP: 47, 59; /Greg Wood/AFP: 30

The RFU Collection via Getty Images: 3; /Steve Bardens: 4-5, 12-13, 19, 21, 75B, 79B, 81B, 85B; /David Rogers: 9, 14, 15, 18, 20, 66B, 67B, 68T, 69B, 70T, 71T, 71B, 72T, 72B, 73T, 74T, 74B, 75T, 76T, 76B, 77T, 77B, 78T, 78B, 79T, 80T, 80B, 81T, 82T, 83T, 83B, 84T, 85T, 93, 102, 103; /Tom Shaw: 66T, 67T, 69T

Every effort has been made to acknowledge correctly and contact the source and/or copyright holder of each picture and Carlton Books Limited apologizes for any unintentional errors or omissions that will be corrected in future editions of this book.

The towering figure of England captain Martin Johnson lifts aloft world Rugby's greatest prize in 2003. Will Chris Robshaw have the honour of lifting the Webb Ellis Cup following the Final of Rugby World Cup 2015?